Nov 16, 2014

Dear Kani & family,

Thank you for your support of this book. I hope you enjoy reading the many stories.

Lord Krishna's Choicest Blessings.

Raj

Living with Purpose

Pt Sirju's Spirited Journey

RAJ PERSAUD

BALBOA
PRESS
A DIVISION OF HAY HOUSE

Copyright © 2014 Raj Persaud.

All rights reserved. No part of this book may be used or reproduced by any means, graphic, electronic, or mechanical, including photocopying, recording, taping or by any information storage retrieval system without the written permission of the publisher except in the case of brief quotations embodied in critical articles and reviews.

The rights apply to the graphic designs of Mud Mathya, Tillak Procession, Clonbrook train station, and, Young Pt Sirju leading India Independence March. The designs were created by Shivaal Misir, Akshay Misir, Tiya Misir and Dhiren Misir respectively.

Balboa Press books may be ordered through booksellers or by contacting:

Balboa Press
A Division of Hay House
1663 Liberty Drive
Bloomington, IN 47403
www.balboapress.com
1 (877) 407-4847

Because of the dynamic nature of the Internet, any web addresses or links contained in this book may have changed since publication and may no longer be valid. The views expressed in this work are solely those of the author and do not necessarily reflect the views of the publisher, and the publisher hereby disclaims any responsibility for them.

The author of this book does not dispense medical advice or prescribe the use of any technique as a form of treatment for physical, emotional, or medical problems without the advice of a physician, either directly or indirectly. The intent of the author is only to offer information of a general nature to help you in your quest for emotional and spiritual well-being. In the event you use any of the information in this book for yourself, which is your constitutional right, the author and the publisher assume no responsibility for your actions.

Any people depicted in stock imagery provided by Thinkstock are models, and such images are being used for illustrative purposes only. Certain stock imagery © Thinkstock.

Printed in the United States of America.

ISBN: 978-1-4525-1786-5 (sc)
ISBN: 978-1-4525-1787-2 (e)
ISBN: 978-1-4525-1922-7 (hc)

Balboa Press rev. date: 08/18/2014

Profits from this book will be used to fund the Pt Sirju P Misir Scholarship Foundation and other Charitable causes.

Contents

Foreword ix
Introduction xiii
Author and Contributors xvii

Chapter 1: Family Beginning, Early Days (1923 – 1943) 1
Chapter 2: Leaving School to Work, First Learning
 About Religion 13
Chapter 3: Marriage 1947 (age 23) 22
Chapter 4: Business 1947 -1959 (ages 24 – 36) 38
Chapter 5: Beginnings of Spiritual Journey 51
Chapter 6: The Rising Priest (Mathya Transformation
 and 7 Day Yajna) 71
Chapter 7: Sirju's Commitment to the Larger Community 96
Chapter 8: Fatherhood, Family, and Grandchildren 119
Chapter 9: Friendships 158
Chapter 10: Leaving Guyana; Canada Days 173

Epilogue 199

Appendix 1: Chelas' Tributes 211
Appendix 2: Contributors 217
Appendix 3: Glossary 219

Foreword

The apple blossom exists to create fruit; when that comes, the petal falls.

— Kabir Das

This book is dedicated to the exemplary life our dad lived. One can easily say without any hesitation that our dad lived as he preached and died as he lived. He was available for others as he so often demonstrated with his interaction with all. In his final moments, his soul departed as some would say as peacefully as he lived.

The 10 children - Raj, Chandra, Anant, Pt Jaiwant, Parbatee, Basso, Shiv, Kay, Hemant and Ravi, and their families, and our dear mother Dalia are inspired by the accomplishments and contributions that our father has made to society. We have ventured on this journey to humbly capture in this book the life and times of our dear father, grandfather and husband with the hope and aspiration that anyone reading this book will be inspired by his life.

I, Ravi, was the youngest of the 10 children of my parents and like my siblings, was fortunate to accompany my father on many occasions. When I was in the tender age group of 8-12 years old, I went along with him on business and social trips as well as on his priestly calls throughout the villages of Guyana. My father loved to help when he could. Even at my young age, it never ceased to amaze me how my father always capitalized on the strengths of the influential and successful people he would come across in his outings, not for his personal gain but to help others who were less fortunate. Through his leadership and unselfish motives, he was able to acquire loans for others so they could make purchases for their families or buy a car to sustain a living, help a youth obtain employment, or arrange many successful marriage unions by liaising between the families. He would intervene in very vicious fights, even when his own life was in danger, in order to protect the victims and the underdogs.

I was always keen in observing the many visitors who would come to seek advice and guidance from my father at our home in Clonbrook Village, Guyana. Our home was the hub for anyone seeking any sort of counsel - be it spiritual, social or business at anytime and any day. One could say my father was a spiritual advisor, family counsellor and healer, and he was exceptional at them all. His implicit faith and confidence allowed all who visited him to leave with a sense of well-being and protection.

Apart from imparting his timeless advice to those around him, my father shared the same wisdom with his 10 children and all his grandchildren. To me, one of his most precious and timeless pieces of advice was a counsel to choose one's friends wisely. He encouraged all who came to him to always associate with friends who will elevate you rather than bring you down. Hence, it was not surprising if you examined the company and the books my father read, they were all of great men. The authors of the books he read until his soul departed, one could say, were his friends. He profusely read the teachings of Swami Sivananda, Swami Jyotirmayanada, Sri Ramakrishna, Swami Vivekananda and other such great saints and sages of India.

A description of my dad would be incomplete without a mention of his humility. He took no credit for any accomplishment or perceived success that came his way. On the numerous occasions when someone praised him for a specific achievement, he quoted the following verse from the Ramayana:

The Lord is the doer; I am just the instrument

Where the devotee Hanumanji, spoke to Lord Shri Ram telling him that everything he (Hanumanji) has acquired or accomplished, emanated from God.

The life examples and stories illustrated in this book, showed that my father's life was a journey punctuated by spirituality, faith, humility, perseverance and kindness.

Sat Chit Ananda (Truth Consciousness Bliss).

Ravi Misir

Introduction

Death is not extinguishing the light; it is putting out the lamp because the dawn has come.
—Rabindranath Tagore

January 2, 2012: the day started off like any other. Pandit (g) Sirju Persaud Misir did his morning meditation, the only difference was that it seemed to last longer than usual. The meditation having concluded, he then changed from traditional attire - dhoti (g) and kurta (g) - into pants and shirt. But while sitting on his bed to pull on his socks, Pt Sirju fell to the ground. He was taken to Markham Stouffville Hospital, Markham, where he was diagnosed with a broken hip.

Two days later he was in great spirits and seemed to be recovering well from the surgery done the day before. He asked his children to bring along some reading material the next day, specifically Joel Osteen's *Your Best Life Now*. It was his last request, for on the morning of January 5, Pt Sirju suffered a massive heart attack and succumbed the same evening. He was 88 years old.

The wake was held for two nights at the Vishnu Mandir, Richmond Hill temple, followed by two nights at the Elgin Mills Cemetery, in Richmond Hill, and cremation the next day. Hundreds of his god children, friends, acquaintances and family attended the wake, where many provided glowing anecdotes eulogising his noble qualities, and describing the immense contribution that he had made in his lifetime.

The tributes described him as "a great mentor whose life was an example for all to follow. He cared about everyone regardless of race, age, religion, sex or political persuasion. A huge part of his life was spent helping people and building communities in Guyana and Canada." People also commented, "his teachings and encouragement to young children were remarkable, as he always made himself available for discussions about the Hindu religion and whatever adversity affected you in spite of the responsibilities of his family and personal life."

In describing their individual relation with him, a recurring sentiment expressed in the tributes was the love and compassion he felt for anyone he met. They praised Pt Sirju's dedication to community and the religious upliftment he carried out with humility. His belief that consciousness was inarguably life's greatest achievement was fondly remembered and admired.

The tributes likened his life to a Gandhi, or that *his godly traits can be seen by the way he walks (so graceful), talks (so softly), smiles, etc.* He was a simple man and would have blushed at these references.

Pt Sirju had a penchant for story telling. At any one time, he unfailingly had an anecdote ready, in which he would recount encounters with one of the many people he met. Related in his characteristically vibrant and emotional style, the anecdotes reflected his empathy for another human being, his zest for life, and his simplicity. The attention to detail in his stories seemed to result from a combination of two other traits: undivided attention to anyone whom he met, treating each person with the utmost deference that also made each one feel like a special friend; and an ability to recall and recount each encounter with great accuracy and flourish. The first must have influenced the second.

The anecdotes invariably included specific discussions he had with the individual he was describing, as he would surely have tried to initiate one. Walking down the road or sitting at the doctor's office were all opportunities for Pt Sirju to attempt to enter a discussion and get to know the people around him. Most often, these discussions resulted in the sharing of useful information on family, philosophy or community events.

He loved a mike (microphone) as one tribute noted, denoting another of his qualities, namely his love of public speaking. Here in the public domain, he demonstrated his vast knowledge of the Hindu scriptures and their relevance to everyday life. He had accumulated this knowledge since his early boyhood and applied it up until the last days. In a private setting, he had the same propensity to hold his listeners captive; with colorful stories of people and events even those long past, culled from memory's banks with an unfailing ability that did not diminish with age.

In October 2011, three months before his passing, the family was returning to Toronto from Queens, New York after attending a 3-day yajna sponsored by his oldest son Anant and family. They stopped at a shopping centre in Buffalo and while the rest of the family scattered about the various stores, Pt Sirju chose to sit out on a bench outside at the mall. As the family was completing their shopping, his son Shiv drove up to tell him that the family was ready to resume the journey to Toronto. He found his father immersed in deep conversation with a middle aged Caucasian lady. Shiv circled the drive to give his father some more time, and then gestured that the family was waiting on him to continue on with their trip. His father motioned back that he needed a few more minutes, and as he was finishing his conversation and walking away from his new found friend, the woman was overheard saying, *it was a pleasure meeting with you Sir.*

On a few occasions such as when he was rebuffed in an elevator as he tried to engage a stranger in a conversation, he kept smiling, and would later recount the incident with humour.

The words of Albert Einstein aptly describe the way Pt Sirju sought fit in the conduct of his life:

> *A human being is a part of a whole, called by us 'universe', a part limited in time and space. He experiences himself, his thoughts and feelings, as something separate from the rest - a kind of optical delusion of consciousness. This delusion is a kind of prison for us, restricting us to our personal desires and to affection for a few persons nearest to us. Our task must be to free ourselves from this prison by widening our circle of compassion to embrace all living creatures and the whole of nature in its beauty.*

Through humility, simplicity and humanity, Pt Sirju fulfilled his life's mission. By his own unfaltering efforts, he was able to rise above the most unlikely circumstances, to make a difference, and inspire all around him.

Upon hearing so many people come forth with praise, admiration, and love, Pt Sirju's family and friends longed for a way to record the impact Pt Sirju had on so many. And thus, the idea of this book was born. They gathered together with the purpose of documenting Pt Sirju's life story for his grandchildren and their kids, his many chelas (g), and the people of his community who he loved. The story is also a lesson in humanity for all.

Author and Contributors

Raj Persaud was the eldest of Pt Sirju's ten children; as such, she served as a 'pioneer' of sorts for the group. She was the first to leave Guyana and the first to study abroad; later, she would play a major role in helping many of her siblings assimilate into North American society.

Although she enjoyed a long, successful career in Information Technology, Raj's interests were not limited to her field. Upon her retirement in 2012 she had yet to fulfill one of her oldest aspirations. More than anything, she wanted to write a book - she had often spoken with her dad about this desire, sadly not knowing that her first book would be on his life.

Raj's wish to write a book comes as no surprise to anyone familiar with her considerable appreciation for both modern and classic literature, yet over the years Raj's book remained unwritten - life, as it sometimes does, got in the way.

Once the idea to put Pt Sirju's life to text took hold, this all changed. Her efforts toward the completion of this book speak directly to the importance of its contents.

In many ways, the life of Pt Sirju was a masterpiece in itself, rich with examples of remarkable benevolence and the kind of selflessness that is woefully uncommon in today's world. All things considered, there could be no better selection for Raj's first literary work.

Her book would finally be written, and fittingly, it would manifest itself as a commemoration of her father's incredible life.

Dhanesh Misir is grandson of the late Pt Sirju and nephew to this book's author. Once the idea to preserve Pt Sirju's life through text completed its evolution from suggestion to undertaking, Dhanesh collaborated with his aunt in the initial stages of structuring and outlining the book.

An aspiring novelist in his own right, Dhanesh lives in New York and visits Toronto regularly, to spend time with family.

Shivaal Misir, Akshay Misir, Tiya Misir and Dhiren Misir, grandchildren of the late Pt Sirju, contributed the four illustrations in the book. The illustrations were used as some of the actual pictures were destroyed in a fire at the family home. The children were tasked to re-create these artifacts and memorable events in Pt Sirju's life history based on information gathered from various contributors. Their creations reflect the enthusiasm with which each delved into their subject matter.

Collecting information from sources spanning five countries and three continents could be described as nothing but challenging. In fact, it would have been close to impossible if not for the individuals who came forward and volunteered to do the digging and tracking down that a project of this nature requires. This book was constructed with factual accounts and recollections at its core; thanks to the passage of years, such information is both scarce and incredibly valuable. As such, this endeavor would have been doomed from the start if not for these individuals:

Parbatee Persaud, third daughter of Pt Sirju, has been instrumental in collecting and documenting stories from family and friends who knew her father well. Parbatee lives with her parents and through her close relationship with her father, she was very informed on all aspects of his life, including the people who were a part of it. Shiv, Hemant and Pt Jaiwant have also assisted in gathering information from members of the community who were close to Pt Sirju.

The book is also a collaborative effort of the Misir family members who include the children listed above, in addition to Ravi,

Basso, Anant, Kaywala and Chandra. They have provided factual details, comments and feedback at each step of writing the book. Without this, and the contributors' willingness to share their stories, the book would be incomplete.

Pt Sirju's numerous godchildren, friends and family provided many of these stories describing their interactions with him. The family appreciates all of the contributions most of which were included in the book. These contributions have been invaluable. The names of all contributors are listed in the appendix.

Dalia, Pt Sirju's wife provided the sounding board for all material contained in the book. Betty, Pt Sirju's sister provided many details surrounding the first period leading into the teenage years of her brother's life. Dr Youtradeo, Pt Sirju's son-in-law, made himself available for discussions on all topics including his experiences in India, and Guyana.

Special thanks to the National Archives of Guyana for providing historical documentation. And finally, many thanks to my editor Corbin Lewars who, by her insightful questions and comments, kept the storyline on track.

> *Books are the treasured wealth of the world and the fit inheritance of generations and nations.*
> – Henry David Thoreau

Chapter 1

Family Beginning, Early Days (1923 – 1943)

A man, as a general rule owes very little to what he is born with – a man is what he makes of himself.
— Alexander Graham Bell

As we trace Pt Sirju's history, it is fitting to begin the story with his mother Chameli. As mothers are wont to do, she was arguably the most influential force that affected the course of his life. The chapter also describes other major influences in his early life.

Chameli, number 83875 on her Emigration Pass, landed on the shores of British Guiana on March 12, 1900 under terms of the Indentured Labour agreement carved by British rulers. She was 6 months old and accompanied by her parents.

Family Beginning, Early Days (1923 – 1943)

Chameli's Emigration Pass

The family's caste, listed as Rajput in the Emigration document, literally means 'son of rulers.' The family originated from the District of Bharatpur, City of Bhosawar, and Village of Randhargar, where Bharatpur is located on the eastern side of the state of Rajasthan.

The documents on indentured labourers describe abhorrent conditions on the boats that took them from their homeland to the colonies. Chameli's parents and Chameli traveled from India to work in the sugar plantations of British Guiana. The boat that brought them suffered from massive overcrowding. The scarcity of food and fresh water combined with the long 3-month voyage resulted in many of the travelers dying from diseases such as cholera and dysentery.

What desperations would have driven parents to undertake such potentially dangerous trip with a little infant in tow? In what was surely an unmistakably massive upheaval from an already irksome life, what was the final straw that pushed them over the figurative edge, in agreeing to a seemingly perilous future? One can only guess that any sadness at leaving their homes, would have been outweighed by hopes and dreams of a strange promised land.

Many men and women survived the treacherous trip in the boats, but could not stomach the pain of isolation from the families left behind. Added to the harsh conditions under which they were forced to work and live in the new land, it is understandable that these few answered the siren call to return to the familiarity and dubious security of their homeland.

Chameli and her parents settled with the majority for whom there was no turning back; continuing on their journey, as turbulent and whimsical as the unbridled winds and currents serving destiny's unrelenting lead, to a land of hope; and dreams of a better life. Having left their motherland with an intent to accumulate wealth and return in a state of financial success, a new perspective like the willful roots of a transplanted tree, took hold. The foreign land was their new home; and to leave what they were now building, would be akin to leaving their home again. Their prior "homeland" now seemed a distant memory; one where they may never again be able to fit in with her people.

Nostalgic, no doubt, they persisted, enduring the cruel realities of the grueling conditions they inherited in the sugar plantations. With an eye to first completing the terms of the Indentured Labour agreement with British masters, they looked ahead to the future with determination.

Chameli completed her indenture-ship term at Plantation Enmore on the East Coast of Demerara. According to records at the National Archives of Guyana, this was performed during her childhood years, although the nature of her tasks has not been ascertained. The material difficulties that she encountered thus far

Family Beginning, Early Days (1923 – 1943)

in her young life did not disappear with the end of indenture-ship. Records indicate that she was married at around age sixteen when she moved to Clonbrook Village on the East Coast of British Guiana to join her husband's family. There she had three sons followed by a daughter in the order: Seecharan, Sirju, Hansraj, and Sukhia also known as Betty. Betty was 6 months old when her dad passed away at age 30 years, leaving Chameli at 29 years old to look after 4 children.

Throughout her life, Chameli demonstrated a fortitude, which included an ability to face challenges head on; and an acute sensibility with an eye for enterprise and upliftment. The extent to which the ability to endure, was a direct outcome of earlier hardships, or was the reason that she survived the hardships, must be left to pure conjecture.

As stated in *The Rajputs of Rajputana* (A Glimpse of Medieval Rajastan) by Dr. M.S.Naravane:

> *The Rajput's love for adventure, great value placed on individual independence, fortitude, presence of mind are some of the qualities that have not dimmed with the passage of time.*

And as described in "Rajputana Discovery, About Rajasthan"
> *The intense pride in their origin and ancestry, intense loyalty to the clan, and intense belief in the righteousness of their cause, made the Rajputs the bravest of the brave.*

During this period in the history of British Guiana, labourers who had completed their indenture-ship terms on the sugar cane fields, turned their attention to rice cultivation. They identified this industry as a perfect opportunity wherein to focus their collective strength and energies, and create an economic future independent of British masters. In the village, many families were acquiring small plots of 2 to 5 acres of land for the purpose to cultivate rice crops.

Rice farming in British Guiana, an industry highly dependent and synchronized to the rainy season, was accordingly confined to two cycles. The major cycle predicating June rains, got underway with plowing the land in May. The cycle was completed in the October to November timeframe, when harvesting, separating the rice from the stalks, and placing it in bags ready to be sent to the rice factory for milling occurred.

Plowing and preparing the land involved use of a juwat (g). This contraption attached two bulls first to a plow, to plow the land, then to a henga (rake) to level it. Once the land was prepared in this manner, a beya (corner plot measuring about twelve by twelve feet) filled with water was selected to set the rice seeds. By June, the swollen seeds had sprouted and grown to 6 to 8 inches. These were dug up and tied into bundles, to be distributed to the women for planting.

The key roles that the women played in the fields, contributing equally alongside the men, demonstrated the great teamwork between the two genders in accomplishing the shared objective of improving their lot. The division of labor capitalized on gender abilities and skills; where the men would perform the hardy tasks of plowing and watering the crops, while the women would provide a female touch through tasks more aligned to nurturing, in planting and harvesting the crops.

Chameli's primary income came from her work in the rice fields, but during the hot, dry season, Chameli fetched dirt for the local burn heap (g), in order to supplement her earnings. Once burnt, the dirt was made into bricks which were used for purposes such as building roads. When this season coincided with that of the rice seasons, she spent the day at the rice fields, the early evening at home to prepare dinner and tend to her children, and then worked at the heap until midnight.

The bravery and accomplishments of Chameli and her contemporaries in the face of tremendous adversity is nothing short of extraordinary. The value system of these pioneers into a foreign

Family Beginning, Early Days (1923 – 1943)

land included the ideals of supreme strength of character, and an unflinching purpose to succeed. How did they endure the difficult lifestyle, and not lose heart and sight of the dream to build a better future? How did they find the resolve to move forward gracefully?

As a means of relaxation from the tedium of village life and to preserve their sanity, Chameli and her women peers enjoyed the perfect antidote through creation of a women's group that relished and shared in celebrations of the villagers' small joys. The peer group included the women with whom she spent the major part of her working life, at the rice fields. Through the shared circumstances experienced at work and play, the group re-enacted the folklore brought over by their parents and entertained the village women with their interpretations through song, dance and humour. The nostalgia of the old traditions - thus transformed - would have brought a touch of familiarity, enabling them to enjoy the old even in their new surroundings.

Their "joie de vivre" spread and became well known in the community, and with the increasing popularity, the group was called to entertain at weddings, birthdays, and nine day (g) celebrations in Clonbrook and neighbouring villages. In addition to a means of relaxation, and having some fun, the group provided a comfort and security of belonging, as well as a support system that would have been invaluable to Chameli.

It would be remiss not to mention the women in the group, who became household names in the lexicon of the village women's leisure pastime. The singers included Tilia, Nellie, Dhanwa, Dunkus Ma, Baeban, Jas (Hoolas), Budhan and Lash Ma. Each singer was known for the special type of folk songs she sang, ranging from wedding songs or sohar (g). Accompanying the singers were accomplished drummers Basiran and Jhugri, with Budhan on the dhantal. Two women Khus Khus Baba and Bhani Ma were natural comedians, regaling their audiences with humorous stories. Chameli herself was a versatile performer, the skills and passion she threw into her performances perhaps telling a tale of endurance and hope.

Father's Passing

Sirju's father passed away in the prime of his life at age thirty, young Sirju was 7. He remembered it as a "happy" occasion, perhaps because he was too young to understand the loss and instead enjoyed the prospect of being the bearer of a newsworthy event, which he was eager to share with anyone who cared to listen. In his long shirt, bare bottomed, and barefeet, he walked to the neighbouring villages of Dochfour and Hope Estates, to convey the news and extend invitation to the wake, announcing happily that tea and biscuits would be served.

This was the only memory he indicated retaining of his father. Unfortunately, even that much is left incomplete, as the cause of his father's passing remains unknown. And though Sirju related the account as an impartial observer, the listener felt a certain sorrow for the little boy, for the loss he described, and for his innocence on the meaning of this loss. Or perhaps the dispassion was a sign of an underlying intelligence that sensed an assurance and faith all his own. The earlier photograph on the back cover shows just this poise that reflects a mysterious self-assurance notable in someone of that young age.

Early Influences

Although he lost his dad at such a young age, his life was not without a father figure. Dipnaraine Paarey had arrived with no family from India as an indentured labourer in the late eighteen hundreds. He later got married to Gujrati, Sirju's phuwa (g). Their marriage broke down, and Gujrati remarried, moving away to the neighboring village of Unity. 'Nandosi' to Chameli, a Hindi term labeling the relationship between a woman and her husband's brother-in-law, the name stuck to Dipnaraine, and everyone including Chameli's children referred to him by the name of Nandosi.

Family Beginning, Early Days (1923 – 1943)

Some time after her husband's passing, Nandosi, already an old man in his seventies, took Chameli's young family under his wings and became the closest semblance of a father figure to Sirju and his siblings. Chameli, for her part, cooked and cleaned for him, and took care of him when he fell ill. Childless himself, Nandosi loved the four children as his own, and he developed a special bond with each of them. In return, through the selfless devotion showered on them, Sirju and his three siblings developed an intense fatherly love for their Nandosi.

He personified the industry of the Indian in his close and intense relationship with the land. Gardening was the passion of his life. Not a surprising fact, considering that the Indian people who were selected as Indentured Labourers and sent to the colonies were chosen to work the land. Like many of them, he developed a great affinity for nature during this process. At early dawn, Nandosi headed to the savannahs (g) where he did his gardening, walking the approximately two miles it took to reach the site of his farmland. The land was replete with a wide variety of vegetable crops that he planted, including pumpkin, watermelon, cantaloupe, squash, tomatoes, banana, and peanuts.

In addition to gardening, he owned a number of cows, as did Chameli. They were all kept on his land at the savannahs, where he milked and tended to them.

Arriving at dawn, he seldom returned home before midnight from labor at his farms, to the worry of Chameli and her family. Sirju—in his early teens during this time and one of the oldest of Chameli's children—often accompanied him to the farm to take care of his crops, and tend to the cows. By learning through action, Sirju was able to self-educate himself. No task was too lowly. Sirju immersed himself in each one that required attention at that moment.

Nandosi, through his industry and dedication, built up relatively considerable wealth and acquired assets in the form of coconut and rice land. His life example illustrates the belief that any labour of love is rewarded manifold. The belief is best described in the following Lao Russell quote:

> *Whatever work you perform with deep desire, God will work with you by doing exactly as much for you as you do to manifest Him. The farmers, or gardeners, or foresters know this. They know that a little work given by them brings but little work done by Nature. The giving and regiving are always equal. The more service you give to Nature, the more Nature will work with you in her regivings.*

Over and above the material support that Nandosi provided the family, by far his most valuable contribution to Sirju's life was inarguably a mentorship that seemed to imbue the boy's mind with notions of possibilities that exist beyond the realm of the physical world. Reading the Ramayana (g) was a regular practice of Nandosi's, and judging from a love of reading Sirju demonstrated even at this young age, he likely experienced his first thirst for learning by witnessing and experiencing Nandosi's recitations.

Through Nandosi's guidance, the young Sirju took up Hindi classes at the local village priest's. Pandit Tribhuwan Maraj detected a spark in the young man, taking him on as his protégé and to be the fire baba (g). He would help Sirju prepare small speeches to deliver to local audiences, but had a tough time getting him to overcome his stage fright and much to his chagrin, the young lad could not summon up the courage at the appointed moment.

Listening intently to Nandosi and his peers discuss social and religious matters and the introduction to study deeply religious texts would have sown the seeds, albeit latent, for Sirju's spiritual seeking.

By the time Sirju was twenty, he had lost two fathers. When Nandosi passed away he bequeathed his worldly acquisitions to Chameli's four children. Sirju received a half portion of home where they resided, plus the house lot abutting it. The residential home was initially owned by Chameli and later rebuilt by Nandosi. One tale relates how the house was rebuilt and paid for with the $600 Nandosi saved from sale of a crop of tomatoes which was sold at 1 cent per pound.

Sirju, much later on, bought the other half of the home, where he lived for the major portion of his life in British Guiana. Nine of his ten children would be born in this home, where his mother lived with him and his family until her passing at the age of sixty six. During her entire lifetime, she and her son enjoyed the same close personal and business relationship. Undoubtedly, much of the mother's sense of purpose and strong work ethic had a tremendous influence on her son.

In addition to the home, all of Nandosi's ancient books were passed on to Sirju. They included spiritual texts that Nandosi had brought with him when he arrived in British Guiana from India in the late eighteen hundreds. Sirju tended them with great care and eventually transported them to Canada during his many visits to Guyana.

Decades later on May 16, 2009 when a fire broke out at the family's Markham, Canada residence, no one was hurt, but the fire caused major damages to the home, requiring the family to find alternative accommodations. All of the cherished books were destroyed and Sirju's grief was immense. At his son Hemant's home, well-wishers dropped by after the fire to offer support to the family, to find Sirju sitting amidst scraps of wet wrinkled paper that he was sunning out in an attempt to save whatever history he could. He could not save the major works as these were all burnt to ashes. Judging from his grief at the loss of Nandosi's books, it is likely that he viewed the event as a psychological severing of an important link to his past.

The works included Nandosi's hard copy of the *Ramcharit Manas Katha Yagna*, a red cloth bound version that saw many a restoration to its well used yellowing and crispy pages, and his hard copy versions of the *Garuda Purana* and *Bhaktivedanta*. In addition to the ancient material that had been painstakingly preserved until the fire, Pt Sirju had amassed his own collection, including a Bible New Testament among other spiritual works and eclectic books addressing varied topics.

Early Influences - Lionel

With his mother Chameli away in the rice fields during most of his pre-teen years, Sirju and his 3 siblings were taken care of after school by the kind women from the Seedhar and George DaSilva families in the village, who bathed, fed and watched over them until their mother arrived from work. They were Georgie DaSilva, and her sisters Marie and Matt Seedhar. Their mother, Grannie Wintie, was of Portuguese descent and their father Seedhar, of Indian descent.

Matt was responsible for bathing the kids. With Sirju, she would scrub him silly, her hope was to make the 'Black Sam' as she called him, white. The other name that she gave him was 'Lionel' sometimes affectionately shortened to 'Nello', a name that stuck until his adult years; as many people refer to him as 'Pandit Lionel', understandably, not a name he relished.

The pseudo-family provided a semblance of normalcy to Sirju and his siblings. It was likely the only time where he experienced the rituals a normal childhood holds, such as being able to play silly games and even being given a nickname!

As we look back at the early influences, we see the immense sway of the positive influences provided by his mother Chameli and father figure of Nandosi, on Sirju's deeply receptive young mind. The combination of fortitude, hope and constant quest for knowledge and improvement exemplified in the lives of the parental figures, could undoubtedly be traced as the forceful beginnings for Sirju's own enlightened journey.

Family Beginning, Early Days (1923 – 1943)

Chameli at 64

Chapter 2

Leaving School to Work, First Learning About Religion

You must live in the present, launch yourself on every wave, find your eternity in each moment.
— Henry David Thoreau

At the age of fourteen, while in fifth standard, Sirju felt a compulsion to shoulder more responsibility in the care of his mother and younger siblings. His distaste for formal tuition along with a sense of responsibility for the family, led him to abandon formal schooling. Much to the chagrin of his mother and his mentor Nandosi, he chose a self-taught alternative, one which he abided by tenaciously until his last moments some three quarters of a century later.

Love, or at the least a liking, of physical labour was not an innate characteristic for him, but weighed against a sense of responsibility, preference lost. His first job with the Sea Defence at the village of Belfield was not his ideal position, but he did not balk at performing his duties. Belfield, situated 4 miles west of the village of Clonbrook was a quiet rustic village. It stretched north of the massive concrete walls keeping the Atlantic waters at bay. A verdant oasis overlooked the ocean. The village acquired claim to fame a few years later when the country's President built his home in this charming, rural neighborhood.

Leaving School to Work, First Learning About Religion

To get to work, Sirju bicycled to the Sea Defence outpost at Belfield village each day. The route wound along the famed 'sea wall'. Its concrete walls—several feet in width and height—bordered the many layered buttress of dense mangrove (g) and courida (g) bushes. They protected these coastal areas, which lay six feet below sea level, from incursions of the nearby ocean. Past this stretch, he wound his way beyond popular local Hope beach and quiet Nootenzuil village to his destination. He was a nature lover and enjoyed the daily trek. Many of Sirju's friends also settled in the area around Belfield, allowing for a sense of community.

At the outpost, he and his work crew were assigned to designated sections of the sea wall along the east coast to tend to any fissures or anomalies that appeared. Despite the physical nature of the task, something that he was not cut out for, he kept the Sea Defence job for four years. Lakharam Jaipargas recounted that his brother who had worked with Sirju at the Sea Defence related that Sirju worked hard at his job. Through endurance, Sirju demonstrated even at this early stage a clear sense of purpose in the choices he made; or at the least a determination to meet the goals he set for himself, even if it meant going outside his comfort zone.

In seeking out and fostering relationships with his much older peers, Sirju was already exhibiting a gregarious streak. His self-propelled foray into adult type maturity and sense of responsibility showed early signs of a leadership flair, especially within the family.

Sirju's younger sister Betty narrated how Sirju was effectual in her marriage. At the Sea Defence, he met Sukhdeo (Bill) Singh, a friend of his employer. Spending a lot of time in each other's company, they became close friends. When Bill married the employer's daughter, Betty and Sirju's mother Chameli accompanied him to the wedding. That marriage unfortunately ended with the death of the bride during childbirth. The newly widowed Bill expressed to Sirju a desire to marry his sister Betty. Sirju approved of the potential liaison, and through his influence, Chameli agreed to the marriage proposal.

Bill and Betty produced two children Jeff and Janet. Bill left Guyana in the early fifties for England when his youngest child was only two years old. He eventually brought his family over to Canada twenty years later, settling in Ottawa. Bill's relationship with Sirju and his family endured the distance and ravages of time. He took great pleasure in welcoming and picking up the relationship where it had left off when Sirju and family later migrated to Canada.

It was an example of the type of tenacious, lasting relationships that Sirju fashioned throughout his lifetime.

After Nandosi

While working at the Sea Defense, he continued with Hindi classes, reading widely, focusing on religious and philosophical books, and accompanying Pt Tribhuwan, his spiritual mentor to various religious functions. His mentor goaded him to try public speaking in the small forums, egging him on with alternating taunts, curses, praise and threats.

At the age of twenty, the full weight of family responsibility came crashing down on Sirju with the passing of Nandosi. Now without a father figure in the family, Sirju was cast in the role in which his older brother showed little interest. In normal circumstances, the oldest son would typically take up the reins, but being the second oldest did not deter Sirju from the duty of helping to sustain the family. Besides showing little interest in taking on these responsibilities, the older sibling knew that Sirju was capable and dependable, as the latter had already demonstrated a sense of responsibility and maturity beyond his years.

In addition to taking on a financial responsibility, Sirju provided emotional support to the family, especially to his mother Chameli. Attentive to her concerns, he always found a way to help alleviate her troubles either by providing advice and support, or by being by her side whenever she needed someone to talk to. He helped with managing and directing family affairs and was available to listen to any of her ideas, comments or questions on finances and family welfare. His mother never made a major decision without first consulting with Sirju. He was also very attentive to her health regime, ensuring that she took good care in food and rest. The two made a formidable team, in the conduct of both business and personal affairs. Sirju maintained this caring and supportive love towards his mother, who continued to live with him until her end.

After Nandosi's passing, Sirju ever alert to whatever winds of change or opportunities showed up, saw a chance to strike out on his own. Through the earnings he had accumulated from his job at the Sea Defence, he bought the two acres of land that Nandosi bequeathed his brother Seecharan and sister Betty. The land was conveniently located at the Clonbrook backdam (g), a short distance from his home. Once again, not deterred by the prospect of demanding manual labour, he took to cultivating the rice land.

Sirju was learning his lessons from the school of experience. The long days toiling at the rice fields provided him with instructions at many levels. They included the honesty of a good day's work in the service of others, as he savored the rewards that came from providing for his family. He enjoyed ample satisfaction in helping his mother whose interests were close to his heart. The feeling of accomplishment validated the principle that his mentor Nandosi's life example taught, that everything is possible if one is willing to put forth the effort and persevere in it. Sirju was proving to be an ideal protégé in his predisposition to eagerly receive instruction and follow in the footsteps of mentors such as Nandosi.

At an early age, Sirju took pride in bearing responsibility and devoting his efforts to help provide for the family unit. He was also learning leadership and technical skills in the process, as well as a greater appreciation of nature. The young years defined a pattern that characterized the rest of his life, where each encounter supplied a life lesson.

Close-Knit Community

In the early to middle nineteen hundreds, the villagers in Clonbrook and surrounding neighborhoods lived harmoniously in close-knit kinship. Hindus, Muslims and Christians coexisted peacefully, treating one another in the manner that members of a large extended family would. The women visited each other's homes whenever there was a family celebration, sharing in the customs and treats that each culture offered.

The liaisons formed as a result of the tumultuous and pell-mell collection of adults and children hijacked and disgorged into the jahaji (g) vessels bringing them from their motherland into the land of the unknown across the mythical dark oceans (kala pani (g)). These liaisons, nourished by shared experiences, have survived through the decades and provided their offspring with an underlying thread of human connection that surpassed religious differences.

These early settlers clung together, deriving support by adopting one another as family. This became apparent at family celebrations. The wedding of Sirju's sister Betty provided many examples of how lasting relationships were forged.

The wedding, performed according to Hindu rites, required a number of roles to be filled in order to complete the ceremony. In addition to the more universal requirements for a father role to give away the bride, there were roles for extended family members. Besides her own children, Chameli lacked any blood relations in the new country. So she needed to assign chosen individuals within the community to perform these roles. In so doing, those selected retained specific relationships, which have carried through to present day generations.

Accordingly, for the mother's brother's role required for the imli (g) ceremony, Hanuman, a close family friend was selected to act as brother to Chameli; Tilia, another family friend was chosen to act as phuwa, and Jasmattie accompanied the bride as the lucknie (g).

Another important relationship that Chameli created was that of a father figure— nana (g) to her children. She adopted Bhagwandin Maraj, a village elder who she respected, for this role, and this gentleman and his family could be depended upon whenever she or her children needed advice or moral support. As was typical of these bonds, they continued with Sirju and the Maraj son, Harry Maraj long after their parents passed on.

Sirju was also close to the men and women with whom he worked on the farms. Many of these, residents from within the community were engaged in the same type of manual labour in the rice and vegetable farms to support their families. Sirju had a down to earth attitude that added a warm personality trait. Armed with this asset, and the empathies arising from a common cause, he formed cordial, enduring relationships with his neighbors at the farms.

Village Pastime

Sirju emerged from his teenage years tempered by life-changing events, which included loss of a father and later of a father figure, both taking place as he completed his teenage years. Shaped by these differentiating circumstances, he was emotionally and mentally mature beyond his years. His demeanor nonetheless conveyed self-assurance impervious to the hardships around him, but there was also a fun-loving side to his personality.

Similar to the manner of his mother who had devised ways to maintain her sanity through the debilitating years of hard labor, he had developed many interests and hobbies which provided necessary balance to a challenging lifestyle.

He had a passion for music and politics; and hobbies included sports such as cricket, boxing, and wrestling. Highly sociable, he enjoyed the evening rituals of hanging out at "the bridge" to connect with his contemporaries in the village to discuss sports and current

Living with Purpose

events, catch up on community goings on, and watch the people going by. Whenever the elderly or sick in the village needed a helping hand, he and his friends would not hesitate to provide assistance.

He kept company with a select group of friends, which included Bill Singh, Raga Raghubir, Doodnauth Raghunandan, and Basil Kowlessar. They hung out together as a group, attending many functions such as weddings, and any village celebrations.

This picture shows him as a twenty-three year old, with two of his friends, Doodnauth Raghunandan to his right and Basil Kowlessar on his left at a baraat (g) they attended at Annandale on the East Coast of Guyana.

Attending Baraat with friends

On another occasion later, Sirju attended the baraat of his close friend Basil Kowlessar in La Jalousie, about twenty miles from Clonbrook. A swami was lecturing at the city hall in the city of

Georgetown, and Sirju did not want to miss out on the lecture. So instead of returning after the baraat ceremony to Clonbrook with the wedding party, he stopped off at city hall to attend the lecture.

He took advantage of every opportunity to uplift himself. As Lord Krishna said in the Bhagavad Gita, chapter 6, fifth verse "A man should uplift himself by his own self, so let him not weaken this self. For this self is the friend of oneself, and this self is the enemy of oneself."

There were many events which had shaped his life to date. In the earlier boyhood days, Sirju had accompanied Pt Tribhuwan Maraj in the priest's rounds conducting pujas. He was also a constant companion to Nandosi, listening eagerly as Nandosi discussed religion and social affairs with his peers. And, he was a student to Nandosi's readings of the Ramayana and other religious texts. This likely influenced Sirju's own love of reading, but it certainly influenced his interest in the Hindu religion.

While all of these experiences in his early life prepared Sirju for a religious awakening, now in his early twenties, he was free to make his own life choices. Attending his friend Basil's baraat, he also accommodated a stopover in order to attend a spiritual discourse, even in the midst of the wedding celebrations. The decision was an example of the choices that he was now making of his own free will, they reflect the spiritual awareness that had taken root.

> *Just as a candle cannot burn without fire, men cannot live without a spiritual life.*
> — Buddha

Living with Purpose

Sapodilla Trees at the Clonbrook Home

Chapter 3

Marriage 1947 (age 23)

For if there is a sin against life, it consists perhaps not so much in despairing of life as in hoping for another life and in eluding the implacable grandeur of this life.
— Albert Camus

The year is 1947 and Clonbrook Village is a peaceful farming village of about a thousand residents nestled cosily between Bee Hive to the east and Anns Grove on the west. A man walking further west would see the village of Dochfour, with its eclectic mix of different races and cultures; then Hope Estates with its more homogeneous population, mainly of Indian ancestry. The inhabitants of the five neighborhoods established a warm and friendly coexistence to create a closely connected hamlet community. The near juxtaposition in terms of their geography and ecology, no doubt, contributed to the close networking connection.

Each of the five communities contributed its own unique flavor to the mix. In Clonbrook, the East Indians, following completion of their indentureships, settled to a comfortable farming lifestyle; smaller numbers settled in Beehive, Dochfour and Hope Estates. To the West of Clonbrook, the village of Anns Grove was inhabited by a people whose ancestors were brought from Africa under arguably more stringent, conditions than the Indians to work as slaves in the sugar industry. By the early nineteen hundreds, they had already broken out of the bonds of slavery and were making a living in agriculture, such as through the coconut oil industry, as well other creative ventures, and living happily, comingling easily with their Indian neighbors to the East.

The Africans and East Indians combined made up the majority, about ninety percent of the population, while the earlier Portuguese and Chinese settlers, and a smaller number of Europeans together with the indigenous Amerindian population made up the remaining ten percent. The groups co-existed rather harmoniously and Chameli's ladies group was invited to perform at many African wedding celebrations. It was a time when the two groups shared and enjoyed one another's culture, sometimes singing together late into the night during these celebrations.

Another contributing factor to the amicable coexistence in the hamlet was a specialization in the goods and services that each group provided. This made for a sociable and unprejudiced use of all resources in the local economy, ultimately adding to a sense of communal well being.

Accordingly, the expertise and focus of the East Indians was concentrated on cultivation of rice and other farm products and on cattle rearing and wage-labouring. The Africans planted ground provisions (g) and fruits such as golden apples, star-apples, genips, coconuts and pamon, and were excellent pastry chefs, specializing in delicacies such as sugar cakes and salara (g). Another lucrative industry, the coconut estates at Bee Hive and Hope Estates provided employment for their local people. The Portuguese and Chinese were the shop owners, providing the retail customer with all their hardware supplies.

The disparate multicultural mix of races provided a model in the integration of ostensibly different value systems. Each still retained their specialties which were cultivated and passed on through many generations, but were also open to the new ideas and strange customs and idiosyncrasies of their neighbours. The inhabitants continued to pursue their daily lives in traditions that had their origins in

Marriage 1947 (age 23)

cultures as diverse as the dissimilarity in ethnicity and geographical boundaries fashioned. However, forces and influences beyond the enclaves of race and culture had now served to unify the communities and create a bustling and vigorous entity.

Neiba (g), get you sweet cassava hey, good price, just for you, was a regular early morning call from an African huckster at the local marketplace where African and Indian sellers gathered every Saturday to spread out their wares and cajole the locals to buy with the offer of a reduced price. A similar holler from the East Indian huckster calling out to their "neiba" and friend to purchase bora (g) and other vegetables, newly arrived by boat from the backdam, created a kaleidoscope of sights, sounds and smells in the early morning crisp pure air, relentlessly beckoning the potential customer to buy.

This was but one example of many common meeting places where the different groups intermingled, showing off merchandise and enjoying each other's company. Another was the annual "greasy pole" race put on by George DaSilva, the Portuguese shop owner. The water sport required that the contestant walk across a greased up pole to the other end of a trench. The one who managed to walk across without falling in the water was rewarded with a prize tied to the end of the pole. The event brought out the adventurous from all races to try their skill and their feat at winning the contest.

Saturday nights epitomized the quiet camaraderie that pervaded the hamlet. It was the time when everyone got decked out to take a stroll to the village marketplace, took time out to smell the roses and forget their problems. Parents sent their children out to visit the market stalls to select a treat: home made ice cream, orange crush drink, sugar cake, and toddy to name a few. Young boys and men gathered around to chat and make plans for the evening, while across the street, the villagers in Anns Grove gathered at Reno Hall for their weekly dance session. The streets buzzed with people of all races enjoying the heady sights and sounds of an evening of leisurely pursuits in the idyllic setting of a rural region yet untouched by any symbols of modernization.

In effect, Clonbrook, and its cluster of hamlets in the early nineteen hundreds, presented a picture perfect model of cultural and racial harmony. This provided the background against which Sirju grew up; imbibing the varied cultural influences which doubtless coloured his view on life.

Clonbrook train station

The illustration shows Clonbrook train station, portraying the semblance of another place of social gathering that characterized all similar depots that dotted the country.

Dalia

Dalia grew up a quiet unassuming girl, no trace of coquetry, amidst a large extended family of uncles, an aunt and their children. She was one of seven daughters and two sons born to Gangadai and Seenanan Tiwari. Her father Seenanan, had arrived at the age of twenty six as an indentured labourer from India in 1912. He arrived alone, unaccompanied by family, to work at the sugar estate at Lusignan,

Marriage 1947 (age 23)

a village neighbouring on Annandale. Throughout his life, he often lamented having to leave all his relatives behind for he missed them sorely. He corresponded with his brothers through letters, but never went back to visit them in India. Dalia's mother Gangadai was a second generation resident in British Guiana, where her parents had arrived from India decades earlier. Dalia and her siblings grew up on Tulsi Dam, Annandale on the East Coast Demerara. Her mother's four brothers and a sister and their children all lived close together at Tulsi Dam, which became the almost exclusive – save for 3 homes belonging to other families - residential enclave of the large extended family.

Seenanan and Gangadai maintained very active, hard working lifestyles for the entire course of their lives. Seenanan when not engaged at the sugar estates where his job included preparing the grounds and planting sugar canes, enjoyed taking care of the cooking at religious gatherings in the community. He was employed at the sugar estate until late into his seventies. Seenanan was friendly and gregarious. In the latter part of his life, after all his children had married and all but the last son had left home, Seenanan's usual post was a seat at the long wooden bench that was installed on the first level of his home. The empty hammock hung beside a bench, inviting family and friends walking by to drop in for chit chat. Family did not disappoint. His home was a usual gathering place for the grandchildren and all the relatives who lived around for social visits to Seenanan and Gangadai, and to catch up with family events. His children and grandchildren talked about the sweets such as badam lachha (g), freshly made, that their dad/grandfather would walk long distances to purchase as treats for them. Among his friends were those who had travelled together in the boat that brought them from India to British Guiana. He would often get together with these jahaji friends to celebrate the various Hindu events such as Holi (g). The festive gatherings brought back memories of the lifestyle they had left behind, but they were grateful to still be able to celebrate in the new country. Seenanan passed away in 1974 at eighty-eight years.

Gangadai, the oldest among her siblings, was a strong spry lady who was constantly on the go. Before marriage, she accompanied her brother Rampadarat to the sugar estates where her job was to tend to weeds among the sugar canes. Later, when the family acquired rice land, she worked in the fields planting and harvesting rice. In addition, she always reared a handful of cows. They provided milk for her family, and any remaining was bought by neighbors. Gangadai would cut and gather the grass from the sugar cane fields to provide food for the cows; she was also responsible to milk the animals. To add to her already full routine, she maintained a large vegetable garden. Gangadai outlived her husband by fifteen years. Even in her eighties, she continued to maintain her household and plant the vegetable garden. She was the sole caretaker of the garden, manually watering the multiple beds of spinach, eggplants, squash and beans, which she sold to the villagers. She enjoyed and took great care of her grandchildren whenever they visited, many of them would stay with her for days during their holidays from school. The grandchildren enjoyed these visits, as their grandmother's kitchen and porch was a usual gathering place for the aunts, uncles and cousins, especially when there was an out of town relative visiting. There was story telling and sharing of jokes as an aunt or uncle took centre stage. One aunt, gifted in story telling, was noted for her vivid and intricate descriptions of the mischievous, nighttime perambulations of 'zombies' (ghosts). The ghost appearances were supposedly witnessed by individuals who could discern these images by virtue of special sensory capabilities. The stories were received with much hilarity by the adults, and wonder and amazement by the children. Gangadai lived a long life, passing away at a ripe old age of 90 in 1989.

Gangadai's brothers were well known throughout Guyana for their dedication to the Hindu religion. Pt Ramsahai Doobay, one of the brothers was a renowned scholar in the religious dogma. Pt

Marriage 1947 (age 23)

Ramsahai's dedication and zeal in studying, practising and spreading the religion was eventually honored with one of the region's highest titles, that of Dharmacharya (g) of the West Indies.

Dalia, like all her siblings, grew up in close emotional connection with her mamoos (g) and mousie (g) and their families. The children played and studied together. Altogether, there were many of the same ages, and they spent all their free time together. They played the usual children's games of hide and seek, hop scotch, and enjoyed other outdoor pastimes. One of these was to hang out at the massive fig tree that stood across the road from their laneway. The manager of the Lusignan sugar estate had built a large wooden seat around the huge tree trunk. All day, old and young gathered under the welcoming shade offered by the widespread obliging branches. Dalia and her cousins were often to be found in the late afternoons picking the fruits and hanging out at the tree. By evening, the children gathered to learn Hindi at the feet of Pt Ramsahai. The entire extended family congregated whenever their spiritual leader, Pt Ramsahai, presided at religious events including pujas (g), yajnas, or family celebrations such as weddings.

Dalia, in addition, spent a major part of her youth keeping company with her widowed nani (g) Sukhdaya, helping her with errands during the day, and keeping her company especially by sleeping over with her at nights. Before going to bed at night, they usually enjoyed a regular routine of evening chat with Pt Ramsahai and his brothers, alternating between their place and his. During this period of spending time with Sukhdaya, Dalia developed a close relationship not only with the grand and feisty old lady, but with her two sons Pt Ramsahai and his brother Pt Ramnarine Doobay; as both sons attended closely to their mother who lived alone.

These were the essence of the social setting within which Dalia grew up, and the unpretentious, and spiritual lifestyle, devoted to family that characterized her early years.

Arranged Marriage

The custom of arranged marriages was one of the many traditions that the Indians brought with them when they landed in British Guiana. Through the years, and with modernization, the custom waned, although it is still practised at varying degrees. In the mid nineteen forties, when Sirju was looking for a bride, the practice was very much adhered to in some segments, especially in rural areas of the Indian population in British Guiana. This was especially true in the family of Sirju's prospective bride Dalia.

Seenanan, Gangadai and her brothers and sister followed the Hindu tradition of arranged marriages, for themselves, their children and those of their siblings. In arranged marriages, a matchmaker studied the backgrounds of the two families. As the marriage was considered to be a union of extended families as well, their values and characteristics must be comparable to ensure a successful union. The belief is that connecting families with similar backgrounds contributes to marital stability. Many children were content to have their parents set up an arranged marriage, (which the parents were delighted to do), as they believed that the parents were well informed on the value system of everyone around in the community. The expectation with arranged marriages is that love will bloom and continue to grow with each day after marriage.

In the case of Dalia and Sirju, a woman from Clonbrook village who knew Sirju well arranged the marriage. Once she met Dalia, she immediately concluded that Dalia would make a suitable marriage partner to Sirju. Her rationale was that both Dalia and Sirju were simple, family oriented and came from a religious background. She introduced the idea of a potential match to the two sets of parents, and after describing the virtues of each of the two young people to the other set of parents, left the matter with them to follow up.

Dalia's family agreed that the young man would be a suitable match and elected her mother's brother Pt Ramsahai to set up a scenario for Sirju to catch a glimpse of his prospective bride. Sirju

Marriage 1947 (age 23)

took along two of his friends to Pt Ramsahai's home and as pre-determined, Dalia walked across the room so that Sirju could see the girl of his dreams. Dalia's parents and all the family were very conservative in believing that members of the opposite sex should not converse. Sirju and Dalia did not talk nor were they introduced to each other that day, but shortly after Sirju's visit, their two families set a date for the wedding.

Tillak

Hindu weddings are elaborate affairs with many events preceding the actual wedding ceremony. One of the most important was the Tillak ceremony, which, sets the stage for the actual nuptials. During the Tillak, male members of the bride's family travel to the bridegroom's home. Once there, the bride's father first places a 'dot' of chandan (g) on the groom's forehead, signifying acceptance of the groom as a suitable husband for his daughter, and solemnizing the coming nuptials. He then presents the groom with the gifts of a wedding ring, cash, and the symbolic dry coconut and sweets wrapped in yellow cloth.

The Tillak party was comprised of members of the bride's retinue dressed in all white clothing. Leading the party were two senior priests, Pt Ramsahai Doobay - mamoo of the bride, and Pt Ramphair Tiwari - the bride's family priest. Both men were well known personalities in the promotion of Hinduism in Guyana. In recognition of their significant contributions, both were appointed Dharmacharya, the highest designation for a Hindu priest in Guyana. The two priests provided an understated dignity by their mere presence. Dressed in traditional white kurta, dhoti and shawl, topped by an intricately wrapped white pagri, headwear of their ancestral lineage, their presence and deportment commanded singular attention.

The sight of the two stately figures descending upon their isolated world would have been enough of a novelty to set the village

Living with Purpose

community abuzz with curiosity and amazement. As if this vision was not enough fodder for curiosity, accompanying the two figures were three other equally tall and imposing men. The three other mamoos of the bride: Pt Ramnarine, Pt Rampadarat, and Pt Ramsaywack Doobay, were similarly dressed in all white kurta, dhoti and shawl.

Rounding up the party, were the bride's father and brother, who were both over 6 feet and dressed in white kurta, dhoti and shawl; the bride's father wearing a simple wrap of white shawl tied around his head. Accompanying the group was Suraj, the nowah (g). He is the smaller sized man carrying a parcel wrapped in yellow cloth in the picture below. He created as much stir, possibly due to the incongruity of his size and dress compared to the rest of the group.

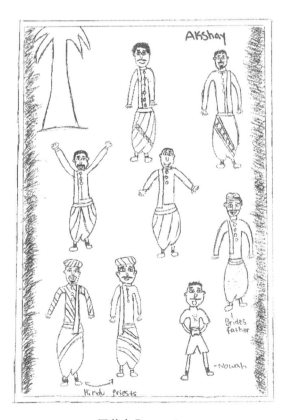

Tillak Procession

Marriage 1947 (age 23)

The group continued past the Anns Grove Methodist school, which in these earlier times, catered to primary school education for children from all races. They passed the old Church adjoining the school, and the village market, hub of village commerce then turned left onto the wooden bridge. While along the route, the villagers looked on with interest. Men and boys hanging out against the bridge rails scampered off the bridge to make way.

Arriving at the groom's home, they were welcomed with the women's group singing appropriate wedding melodies. In the tradition of their ancestors, the ceremony began with offerings to God for his continuing blessings in the new alliance. As was customary, the sounds of gunfire staged by the groom's family announced the joyful conclusion of the first part of the proceedings, and anticipation of the next. It marked the moment where the groom—with outstretched hands—is about to accept the bride's father's gifts of wedding ring, cash, and sweets. The event concluded with refreshments.

The Tillak symbolizes acceptance and wishes of prosperity for the two parties and the families' impending union. It provides an auspicious footing on which the newly weds will start their new life together. The custom, currently no longer followed in its previous form among Indians in Guyana, nevertheless has been integrated with the Engagement ceremony of the bride and groom, to include its original purpose.

The spiritual beginning and colorful end to the Tillak as official start of the Hindu wedding celebrations, foretold an excellent omen for the next sixty five years of blissful marriage life for Sirju and his bride!

Wedding

A week later, on February 11, 1947, on a balmy Tuesday evening, Sirju 23, and his bride Dalia 16, exchanged marriage vows.

Sirju's large retinue of baraatis (g) included close friends: Basil Kowlessar, Doodnauth Raghunandan, Bill Singh, and Raga Raghubeer. This group of friends were close associates with whom he spent time and attended social events. Basil passed away while in his fifties, but many of his children eventually chose Sirju as their guru (g), maintaining a filial relationship with him. The close association that started with their father did not diminish with his passing.

George DaSilva, prominent village Portuguese shopowner, also joined the baraatis. George's family, the Seedars, were caretakers of Sirju when as a child, his mother was away working, and the family stayed close watching over Chameli and her children. As Sirju had a very amiable personality, making friends easily, many of his friends from the village joined the baraatis.

Travelling in about a dozen vehicles, the baraatis arrived at the village of Annandale stopping alongside the main thoroughfare. Gathering at the adjoining Tulsi Dam road, the lively and rhythmic sounds of their tassa (g) drums unmistakably announced arrival of the groom's party. Adding to the fanfare of drums, the baraatis put on a brilliant display of fireworks, as they prepared to welcome the bride's retinue.

Coming to meet the groom's party at the head of the Tulsi Dam road, the bride's relatives responded in kind with tassa music. The procession was lit by the moon in the last quarter and by the dancing red and yellow flares from masaal (g) wicks carried by the bride's relatives.

The procession of groom and baraatis was escorted to the bride's residence to the sound of tassa drums and then was taken along the Tulsi Dam road. Along the road, they passed the homes of the bride's family members, who lived along the perimeter of a close circle spanning both sides of the road. The first home they walked past belonged to Pt Ramsahai, then past the small home of Sukhdaya, followed by the home of Pt Ramnarine, before reaching the bride's residence. Beyond was the home where her mousie Sanjhari lived with her family, while Dalia's two other mamoos Ramsaywack and

Marriage 1947 (age 23)

Rampadarat lived across the canal spanning the Dam. The living arrangements belonged to a time of an era past, when large extended families lived close to each other through necessity, in order to survive.

Darkness had descended by the time the baraatis and their hosts reached the bride's residence, around 7pm. The night sky glistened with a myriad of lights and warm breezes emanating from the nearby Atlantic, which filled the air with fragrant scents of bougainvilleas, frangipani, gardenias and jasmine. A magnificent backdrop for any festivity, it is easy to understand the allure of the evening as the perfect time in which to celebrate a wedding.

At the bride's home, the ladies group was regaling their audience with the appropriate wedding songs, while the groom was treated with the traditional greeting (parche) (g) and aarti (g). The wedding ceremony was conducted according to Hindu rites. Hindu wedding rituals require collaborative family involvement and are designed to strengthen the union of the two individuals by increased stakeholder interest in the marriage.

In the absence of his biological father, Sirju's older brother Seecharan played the father role; Raga Raghubeer, a close friend played the role of elder big brother, and Hanuman once again, acted the role of mamoo. Sukhdeo Singh, married to his sister Betty filled the brother-in-law role. This situation where families did not have blood relatives to fill the various roles was not uncommon. Choosing someone to fill a role, was a carefully thought out process, as the person would be committed to the relationship for life. In this manner, families adopted each other in specific relationships, and acquired support by leaning on one another.

Leaving Annandale

Dalia's leave of her family at Annandale was bittersweet. She recalls that Gangadai started to cry weeks before the departure of her daughter in marriage. Dalia also had a poignant memory of her two mamoos, Pt Ramsahai and Pt Ramnarine, with tears as they bid her goodbye on the day of her departure to the groom's home. She had become an integral part of their lives, and although they were happy for her, and had blessed the marriage, like a daughter going away from the home, it was sad to see her leave.

Dalia related that the first time she saw her husband was when she arrived as a bride at his home in Clonbrook. She was sixteen years old.

Sirju's mother Chameli did not wear much jewelry, but she always wore a heavy silver anklet, known in Guyana as a 'foot ring'. The anklet was passed on to her from her mother who descended from the Rajasthan province of India, where the women wore the anklet as costume adornment, and as a show of bravery as a tribe. In Hindu weddings, it is customary for the groom's parents to provide the clothing and jewelry with which to dress the bride on her wedding day. Included with the jewelry that Chameli sent for Dalia to wear, was her ancestral anklet. Dalia remembers that, to her relief, one of the first things Sirju did on her arrival was to remove the ankle ring. The heavy anklet was not a usual piece of costume ornament that was worn by younger people in British Guiana, and Sirju's taste in jewelry as an expression of contemporary culture obviously differed from his mother's.

On the lighter side, the wedding must have provided fun for the villagers. Latchman Kissoon remembers the ceremony fondly. He said, "It was a treat I will never forget 'Nello wedding mek (make) de (the) village bright'".

Marriage 1947 (age 23)

Newly Weds

This picture was taken at the ACME Studio in city of Georgetown one week after the wedding. No picture of the actual wedding day exists.

The words of Rumi sum up the unconditional love that blessed the union for nearly 65 years.

> *And still, after all this time, the Sun has never said to the Earth,*
> *"You owe me."*
> *Look what happens with love like that.*
> *It lights up the sky.*
>
> *— Rumi*

Pt Sirju and Dalia at their 50th Wedding
Anniversary Celebrations, Vishnu Mandir

Chapter 4

Business 1947 -1959 (ages 24 – 36)

> *He that looks at another human with love and affection without malice and pride, that devotee is near and dear to me*
> *– Bhagavad Gita*

The Crown (or transport land) in Clonbrook, where the Indian labourers settled, extended from the sea wall bordering the Atlantic in the North, to three quarter miles South inland. Stretching beyond, the area known popularly as the savannahs consisted of farmland (or cultivation lands) extending another three miles or so (3.2 miles actually). The leased savannah lands continued for a further half mile ending at the Crown dam.

In its initial state, the savannahs were a mere jungle covered in lush greenery ranging in sizes from large coconut, wallaba (g), greenheart (g) and purple heart (g) trees to the smaller shrubs and grasses. Besides the wild vegetation, a large assortment of tropical fruits including mangoes, papaya, as well as wild fruits such as monkey apple and jamoon grew in abundance. Beyond the savannah and Crown dam, a one and a half mile of lush, unoccupied 'open savannah', stretched to the Conservancy dam. This dam formed a final bulwark to the Conservancy and framed a reservoir that provided the entire East Coast Demerara with fresh water supplies.

Tigers, snakes, and deer, as well as dangerous alligators and camoudie (g), made their homes in the natural forest and littered its swamps. No one ventured forth without advance scouting of the area and with an escape plan in case danger approached.

The villagers instinctively took to the savannah lands for it possessed the key resource that would support their quest for financial and economic success. No stranger to the task of working the land and molding it to suit their purpose, the early settlers were blessed with the courage to take on the daunting challenges of clearing and transforming it.

Winston Churchill affirmed that, *Courage is the first of human qualities because it is the quality that guarantees all the others.*

Armed with such courage, and the enthusiasm and mind-set born out of necessity, these early settlers, including Sirju's Nandosi, painstakingly cleared and gradually transformed their small allotment of the savannah lands into fertile grounds ready for rice and vegetable crops. As a young boy, Sirju helped look after the cows and accompanied Nandosi while tending his vegetable garden. Consisting of a flat terrain of lush green grass, the savannahs provided the animals with an abundant food supply. The cows were left there to graze and roam freely, the owners secure in the knowledge that the animals would be well fed; and even if they wandered off, they would be easily located within the perimeter of the large expanse of land.

Sirju occasionally slept in the outdoors in the savannah while the cows roamed. He fondly remembered how he would pass his days by swimming across the Mahaica Creek with his cows. He would hold onto the tail of one of the cows and within a "whiz" he would be on the other bank of the creek.

The milking cows were housed closer to home and each morning at 4 a.m., Sirju started his one mile walk to milk these cows. He took this task as seriously as any other he encountered, leaving nothing to chance. In one occurrence, he returned home after completing his work at 2 a.m. He had unwittingly gone at midnight thinking it was dawn!

Swami Sivananda's words describe the manner Sirju approached life: *Put your heart, mind, intellect and soul even into your smallest acts. This is the secret of success.*

Following the milking, he fetched the milk home, to hand over to his mother who would then handle the selling. Sales from the usual 2 gallons of milk at 3 cents per pint, provided the family a regular albeit tiny income.

Savannah as Spiritual Inspiration

The backdam and savannah lands provided the resources that contributed to the economic and financial evolution in the lives of Sirju and his parents as second and first generation settlers respectively. However, there was another no less important characteristic of these lands that appealed to Sirju; and that was the inspiration that he found in the beauty of these natural surroundings.

Food, shelter, and communion with the beauty of nature were all available at no cost. The choices in food were limitless: ripe purple jamoon, and orange coloured monkey apples dangling invitingly over the water's edge, brushed by the passerby travelling in their boats or crayols back and forth to the backdam. They entreated all who went by to stop and savour their offerings. A few feet away from the water's edge luscious ripe mangoes of endless varieties, decadent sugar apples, white lady guavas, five-fingers, genips, golden apples and sugar cane could all be found. There were others: watermelons dug into holes and covered surreptitiously to avoid detection; or banana trees heavily laden with large bunches of the fruit; or star apples with their juicy mauve tinged fleshy fruit. To quench the thirst, coconut trees bearing bundles of coconuts, were readily available, providing its cooling liquid and soft sweet jelly. And if one needed a shelter from the rains or the sweltering tropical sun, a thatched roof was easily assembled from woven coconut tree branches. Finally a dip in the cool refreshing clear black water trench (g) was enough to wash away any traces of fatigue and worry, both physical and mental.

Sirju found inspiration from the simplicity and serene beauty of this natural setting. He was preparing to become a pandit and the environment in the savannahs where he tended the cows or worked the rice fields was a nature lover's delight.

Thakur Persaud, a close family friend remembers Sirju in his early twenties: *Going to milk the cows in the backdam early in the mornings and late in the afternoons were his best times to rehearse the mantras (g) and sing his bhajans. He was determined to succeed.*

The scene is reminiscent of the American author, poet and philosopher of the mid nineteenth century Henry David Thoreau. He described his experience in Walden Pond—an experiment to experience nature by living in the woods for two years—as such:

> *I went to the woods because I wished to live deliberately, to front only the essential facts of life, and see if I could not learn what it had to teach, and not, when I came to die, discover that I had not lived...*
> – Henry David Thoreau, Walden: Or, Life in the Woods

While the savannah was a source of peace for Sirju, it was not a very lucrative standby to support a large family. As such, he was always looking for something else.

Growing Entrepeneur

George DaSilva ran a successful hardware and liquor store across the village road on the Anns Grove side of the hamlet. His wife's family, the Seedhars, mentored and befriended Sirju and his siblings from an early age. George offered the use of a small structure stationed on his land for Sirju and his mother to start a business. It was a break that provided Sirju with an opportunity to test his business skills.

Business 1947-1959 (ages 24 – 36)

With his mother at the helm, they opened a small cake shop (g), selling cakes of different kinds that included nuff-nuff, pine tart, coconut buns, salara and tennis rolls. They also offered crushed-ice dipped in syrup; soft drinks; parched nuts and Chameli's homemade mauby (g). Thakur Persaud, a patron and visitor to the shop said of the drink: *The mauby was a real hit, it popularized the cake shop so much that people from all walks of life would crowd the shop on Saturday nights to have a good draught of Chachi Bebe's mauby.* (Chachi Bebe was the name given to Chameli by patrons of the shop, a name that stuck to her).

Dalia, supportive and always by the side of her husband and mother-in-law in every endeavour throughout all their lives, quickly learned the secret of her mother-in-law's mauby drink recipe. While Sirju and his mother ran the store, his wife's contribution consisted in making batches of the drink which she carried to replenish supplies. On Saturday nights, the busiest time for the business, she made and took to the shop snacks such as bara (g), channa with mango and tamarind sauces, sugar cake, and freshly parched peanuts, items that were popular with the clientele.

Working beside his mother in the business, Sirju gave all appearances that he enjoyed this method of commerce. It was a good introduction to the world of grocery business. It also advanced an entrepreneurial spirit which had surfaced earlier when he left his salaried Sea Defence job in order to purchase and cultivate his own rice land. And it was a conduit to steer him away from the more physical field work.

The popularity of the business spread, and at the same time, his family was about to grow with the expected birth of his first child. To make it easier for his mother and wife to mind the shop as needed, he relocated the business to the main floor of his home. The arrangement would free up his time so that he could be away from the store more often as he had many plans for each waking moment.

After the renovation to convert the bottom flat of his home to a full fledged store was completed, there was no cash left to do the painting. Jagoo, a close friend from the community, offered to help Sirju with painting the store. Acquiring a loan with interest from a money lender, Sirju was able to purchase the paint. He and his accomplice Jagoo then proceeded with the painting. It was an amateur job, but a splash of paint always helps, even if there was one too many splashes added, in one too many odd places!

Once they transferred the items from the old shop at George DaSilva's premises to the new location, the store was open for business. At first, it was a mere transfer of the cake shop from one location to another, and the scope of the business remained the same. As the business continued to thrive, Sirju added a new section that offered a wide assortment of the standard grocery items. His mother and wife worked by his side and managed the store when he was away making purchases.

Sirju was as much at ease behind the counter tending to customer's needs; or making the weekly shopping trips to wholesalers in the city of Georgetown, or purchasing groceries to stock up the store. He also took care of the accounting for the store. Working behind the counter at the grocery store meant that commodities such as sugar and flour kept in large barrels needed to be weighed and wrapped in brown paper parcels. To make the parcel, first the top of the paper would be rolled, then the sides, and then weighed with the old scales. Elbows deep in the flour barrel as he catered to the customer's need, he found time to simultaneously initiate a lengthy conversation; one that invariably started with him enquiring after the health and well being of the customer's family. It was his trademark characteristic - always wanting to reach out to the other person.

While he held himself at only the highest standards in fairness and honesty in his business dealings, he also had a keen eye for unscrupulous merchants. Sirju discovered that the numbers weren't adding up when the kerosene merchant filled up the storage tank. To investigate, he diverted the kerosene to two 48 gallon containers. Although he had been charged for 140 gallons, only about 96 gallons

Business 1947 -1959 (ages 24 – 36)

were supplied! And this had been going on for a long time. Sirju, not one to allow an unfair practice to win the day, confronted the vendor. The man denied any misconduct, but ceased the dishonest routine.

Sirju could not send anyone away who could not pay. His accounting principle seemed to be based on the theory of allowing as much debt as possible. If someone came to the store and said that they didn't have cash to pay today, he would gladly give them the groceries and file a note that they would pay at a later date. He never turned anyone away for their lack of ability to pay. So the list of debtors, evident from the increasing slips of paper on the makeshift wire file made from clothes hanger, grew at a rapid rate. There were many different situations that presented themselves where the customer would beg to trust (g) the current expenses, promising to pay the next time. Many of these types of customers would then disappear after a few times of using this promise, likely moving on to another establishment to start the same process all over again, and leaving their trail of paper slips. They promised to pay eventually, but the slips on the wire file grew!

At times it seemed to be more of a philanthropic organization than a business because he was ready to offer assistance to anyone needing it. Interestingly by contrast, he would pay in cash, and in full whenever he made wholesale purchases from vendors. This in addition to the expense incurred from travelling the considerable distance to the city where he purchased much of the store's inventory, ate into the profits of the store.

Later on when he was the village priest, a yajman (g) would ask him to take the sarjam (items required for the religious offerings) from the store. The yajman was expected to pay for the items, along with the dachna (payment for his services), but often forgot to include the cost with his payment, and sometimes forget the payment itself! However, Sirju never requested pay, or reimbursement.

In spite of his generosity and readiness to accept customers' promises to pay in lieu of actual payment, or maybe because of it, the business prospered! The grocery business remained a main source of regular income that, for many decades, continued to support his large family.

His trust and business loans practices led to some interesting and sometimes amusing situations. One such situation involved two villagers having the same name, one of whom owed a considerable debt. The debt amount was rising at a frantic pace, and cajoled by his family, Sirju wrote a note addressed to the debtor, asking for some measure of repayment. His son Jaiwant, a boy of seven at the time, was sent to deliver the note. Returning home, his mother drilled him in an effort to confirm that the note had been correctly delivered. He assured her that he "gave it to the man (him) self". A few minutes after, the man came running to the store with slip in hand, anxiously stating "Pandit, me na owe you money!" The son had delivered the note to the villager with the right name but it was the wrong of the two villagers!

A more shrewd villager had built up hundreds of dollars worth of credit, never paying on any of it. She arrived at the store one day, announcing that she needed to "talk to pandit" about something. It turned out she wanted to open a new credit line! The woman had a poor reputation in the community in terms of trustworthiness and unfortunately added to that, it was believed she suffered from a drinking problem. She was looking for a new line of credit, as she said to "turn over a new leaf." At that moment, she truly believed in her mission. She believed that she was ready to change her ways for the better; but everyone around found the request to be funny. The fact that she even thought that she had a viable request, which to the impartial observer was blatantly over-the-top, tells a great deal about the approachability of Sirju, the man who owned the store. On the other hand, there were many excellent customers who paid their bills regularly. But the above examples illustrate his trademark generosity and compassion.

Harold Kowlessar, the son of Basil, whom Sirju was close to as a young man, has this pleasant memory of Sirju at the store: *A weekly highlight for us was going to his shop to purchase the weekly supply of groceries. Often times, we would be lucky to see him behind the counter,... tall, distinguished looking, always with a warm beckoning smile. You felt at home immediately. Money or not to pay on the spot,.. our list was always fulfilled.*

The store provided a common meeting ground for old and young, who came to shop but always dallied for some conversation. On a number of occasions, the store served as a refuge for younger people caught in dubious circumstances.

A few village boys were in the habit of teasing a gentleman who worked at his vegetable garden directly across from the shop. One afternoon, seeing some boys at the store, the man rushed in waving a machete menacingly, demanding of the youngsters, "so what will you do now?" The boys were not planning on hanging around to find out what he was going to do next. They clambered up the shop's counter making a quick exit through the back door.

On another occasion, a villager suffering from a form of mental disorder ran into the shop, again with a machete in hand. As he waved it, he demanded "who own that big yard?" The "big yard" he was referring to was owned by Sirju (it is described later in the book), but, cowed by the brandishing weapon, no one responded. After repeating his question a few times and receiving no response, he declared that since no one owned it, "I own it." And with that, he took off to the yard and picked a large bunch of bananas. He later apologised for the incident.

A prominent young businessman from the area came to the store one day looking for Sirju, a pandit by this time. The visit would not have created a stir under normal circumstances, except that the man was shirt-less and seemed intoxicated. When Pt Sirju's wife told the man that her husband was officiating at a puja, he wanted the details, such as where, and at whose place the puja was being held. Later in the day, when Pt Sirju came home, he reported that the man went to the home where he was officiating wearing only a towel wrapped around his waist!

During one of the trips to Georgetown to conduct business for the grocery store, two boys approached in a menacing manner. Sirju put his right hand behind his back, and used his hand as if beckoning to a friend at the back. The motion was made so that the potential assailants could see that he was calling someone, but done in a manner where he gave the impression that he did not want them to see that he was doing it! Tricky! On another trip, Sirju spied a potential robber approaching him. Thinking quickly, he pretended there was a friend nearby and started gesticulating to this invisible friend. It was this type of street sense which saved him from harm on many occasions.

Real Estate Dabbling

His first real estate venture proved that he had a special talent for identifying lucrative real estate deals. He bought a massive dilapidated structure destined for demolition on Vlissengen Road, a run-down part of city of Georgetown. Excited with the purchase, he invited a close friend to offer an opinion. His friend was quite unimpressed, stating that the cost of $3000 was too high for a "piece of junk" as he described the building.

Soon after, an acquaintance passing by, and surprised to see Pt Sirju standing beside the building, wanted to know what he was doing in this curious location. On explaining that he just bought the building, the acquaintance immediately asked if he was interested in selling specific parts. Now very anxious to part with the "junk", he offered the fellow a $1000 reward if he could find someone to buy the parts for $5500. The acquaintance left promising to return in an hour. The acquaintance returned with a deal, and Sirju made a profit of $1500 in one day. And thus, a real estate "dabbler" was born. He clapped his hands in mock merriment and in the language of Guyanese colloquialism, "took the money and burn tires."

Business 1947-1959 (ages 24 – 36)

As the old building was being torn down, large segments of material that weighed hundreds of pounds needed to be moved and stored. Finding people able and willing to lift these large chunks was difficult, but searching from village to village, he managed to find laborers to do the job. Using his ingenuity, he utilized the materials from the building to aid in the construction of two new houses.

Maybe his biggest real estate conquest was the "big yard" in Clonbrook that he purchased much later. Originally owned by the sugar estates, it was acquired by the Kissoon patriarch, Sri Kissoon, who built a home on the property, from where he managed his coconut estates at Bee Hive. After him, his son Balmeek Kissoon, a businessman, lived on the property, eventually selling it to Pt Sirju. By the time Pt Sirju acquired the land, it was a prime piece of village real estate, perched in an enviable central location. The view from the front faced directly across to the Atlantic Ocean where at high tide, one could see the waves crashing over the sea walls from the veranda. At the back, the property faced the "middle walk", a large black water basin that fed into the canal leading into the backdam and savannahs.

In the days of the sugar estates, the canal was used to fetch the sugar canes by pontoons from the fields to the factory. When Pt Sirju acquired the property in the late nineteen sixties, it had very rich soil, with fruit and vegetable trees growing in abundance.

It was his best real estate purchase yet. He chose this venue to build a larger home for his family. At this time, he lived with his wife and ten children, as his mother Chameli had already passed on. Pt Sirju derived immense pleasure in planting and nurturing new fruit and vegetable trees such as sapodilla, breadfruit, plum, and avocados among others in the yard. He tended the old trees with as much care by removing parasitic vines and old branches and keeping them looking pristine. He also loved picking the fruits himself – sapodillas, breadfruits, avocado, and mangoes. He had no qualms about using a machete to weed the bushes around the trees to keep them healthy. It was a ritual which he enjoyed; and his hard work showed with the prickly wild flowers that stuck to his clothing when he emerged from one of these ventures in the yard.

The setting was an ideal place to build a home, especially for a man like Sirju who loved the beauty and simplicity of nature.

> *Everything comes to us that belongs to us if we create the capacity to receive it.*
> – Rabindranath Tagore

Business 1947 -1959 (ages 24 – 36)

Breadfruit Trees at the Clonbrook Home

CHAPTER 5

Beginnings of Spiritual Journey

I slept and dreamt that life was joy. I awoke and saw that life was service. I acted and behold, service was joy.
— Rabindranath Tagore

It would appear that all his life, Sirju's experiences to date were being orchestrated by an invisible hand. At the age of 23, the hand guided him to a lifestyle that would fully illuminate the paths his footsteps led. Lao-Tzu, the ancient Chinese philosopher of 500 BC, describes in one of the 81 verses of the classic text, the Tao Te Ching (or the Great Way), that this is exactly what happens when one allows the nameless Tao (God) to take control of one's life. The verse describes the mastery of the Tao, which through its simple and subtle influence directs each individual towards actions for a fulfilled life. Conversely, going against this influence results in a life of frustrations. To quote a section of this, the 32nd verse:

> The eternal Tao has no name
> Although simple and subtle,
> No one in the world can master it.

Sirju's days leading up to his twenty third year never lacked for an industry, albeit one begot of necessity. Whatever duty or activity he was required to perform, he took on unflinchingly, with no fear or anxiety, but with a calm determination that it was the right activity for that moment. He allowed the 'eternal Tao' (God), to guide his every action. But in his twenty-third year that calling seemed to be one of service rather than of industrial labour. He was seemingly fully groomed for this calling and it was a perfect match to his energies and spirit.

Sirju's readings, studies and quests for spiritual insights to date seemed to be leading him in the direction of priesthood. However, he needed a catalyst, one that could help clarify any remaining doubts, and propel him to see clearly where his future lay. The catalyst came from a few senior members of the community who were close family friends. Hanooman was one of the more vocal of these friends. He believed that Sirju had demonstrated the essential qualities that a priest should possess. Other members such as Jagoo and Manoo joined in with Hanooman to persuade Sirju. They pressed that since Sirju was now married to someone who came from a family of Hindu priests, he would easily access any guidance he needed. Together the members convinced Sirju to follow the natural trajectory of his interests and begin training to become a Hindu priest. His guru Pt Ramphair Tiwari, who had been a major proponent of him taking up the priesthood, applauded his move, and Dalia's family approved the new direction of Sirju's life.

Spiritual Mentors

Driven by an insatiable appetite for knowledge, Sirju had always been alert to opportunities to pick up information or guidance towards enlightenment. His spiritual mentor now was the learned Pt Ramsahai Doobay, his wife's mamoo. Pt Doobay, himself self educated, passed on ancient prayers, and formats of rituals. Sirju learned from the best teacher. To make the most efficient use of his and his mentor's time, he would prepare his notes beforehand, and then seek guidance and clarification using his notes as the basis. He spared no pains to absorb the teachings of his mentor. Years and decades later, the bhajans (g) and chants, as well as melodies learnt from the venerable priest became some of Sirju's trademark as well.

Sewdharry, a visiting thinker from India, was introduced to Sirju as someone well versed in the Hindu scriptures. Quick to recognise that here was someone from whom he could learn a lot, Sirju invited the man to be a guest at his home, as had been his practice often times. The expectation was that the visitor would pass on a great wealth of his knowledge on the scriptures during the stay. To Sirju's amusement, his guest did pass on information to him, however he was adamant that he do it in a sparing way. He only provided Sirju with one sloka (g) per day, and no more! A result of this slow knowledge release process was that Sewdharry's stay lingered on.

In addition to seeking out company of the wise and learned, Sirju searched for any reading material on Hinduism, spirituality and philosophy. His voracious appetite for reading remained with him until his last days. To bolster his accumulating knowledge of the philosophies of his religion, he attended the occasional religious classes in the city of Georgetown, Guyana making the best use of any free moments. Throughout his life, Pt Sirju's quest for knowledge never ceased. He received the certificate of competency in Karmkand and Purohit-Karm after having been examined by the Guyana Pandit's Council in June, 1978. His aim was continuous development, to be a better Pandit, and to do the best he could at any endeavour he took on.

With the skills that he was acquiring and constantly updating, he was ready to start the priesthood duties of conducting pujas, jhandis (g) and weddings in the village and surrounding areas.

Beginnings of Spiritual Journey

Early Days As A Priest (Age 24)

The picture depicts him as poised and regal in his priest outfit at one of the first pujas in Clonbrook. It didn't take him long to become an expert at the dhoti-tying, a skill that he lacked earlier. He also wore the traditional outfit with a cool poise, even though it was alien attire amid the heterogeneous cultures in his rural community.

Pt Sirju, the Hindu priest was born.

The diligence and focus of Pt Sirju's studies of the puja and mantras were evident in the disciplined and skillful manner he conducted the sessions. But his generous spirit is what allowed him to take his knowledge and transfer it into an inspirational sermon which reached many people. People in the community enjoyed the sermons and the explanations, as he delved into the colorful poetry of the Hindu slokas and mantras, delivered in his uniquely melodious and passionate style. He was living in the moment.

Pt Sirju's self education continued through studies and conversations, and his popularity increased. He was considered "a likeable priest with a strong melodious voice" and developed a larger reputation for the many qualities and contributions to his community such as family counsellor and social worker.

Marches – India Independence & Hindu-Muslim March

On Tuesday June 3, 1947, the year that Sirju was married, British Viceroy Mountbatten announced the plan for separating India. Pakistan was founded two months later on August 14. One day later, on August 15, India was granted independence. The events across continents touched the lives of Indians all over the world, as it did the peoples of the little nation of British Guiana.

Pt Sirju, a young man of twenty three, was embarking on a parallel course. Only five months into married life, his public life was also about to take off. The village with its predominantly Muslim and Hindu population had so far enjoyed a peaceful and mutually rewarding coexistence. While independence of the two states of Pakistan and India from British rule was a source of pride for the peoples of the village, the violence that erupted in the now two states was no secret to the rest of the world.

In Clonbrook, the Hindus and Muslims—especially the first generation settlers who had arrived as indentured labourers—could not contain their joy at the freeing of their mother nation from British rule. It was a shot in the arm for all these people, who felt that they had suffered untold indignities at the hands of the British. The need for a leader became apparent, as the Hindu community in Clonbrook was now looking for someone to lead them through the changing times. The young Pt Sirju, at twenty six years old, took up the challenge. Latchman Kissoon, Barrister at Law from neighbouring Bee Hive, and a young man at the time, remembers the occasion:

> *It was soon after, in 1950 that Pt Sirju came to prominence as a young leader in the village. On the 15th day of August that year, and in the following years, he led the Indian youths in a revolutionary march from one end of the village to the other singing India's National Anthem and revolutionary songs such as Dur Hatho Dur Hatho Duniya Walo Hindustan Hamara Hai; (loosely translated, it says: please stay away and let us manage our own affairs).*

The villagers, including Christians, turned up to join the march. Leading the large contingent of men, women and children, Pt Sirju headed the procession as they started at the location of the Clonbrook Hindu Temple. To show their love and friendship with Muslim brothers, the group was led to the village market square where they met and embraced the Muslim contingent before continuing the procession through the village streets.

The philosophy of Kabir Das was one that he embraced: *I am not a Hindu, Nor a Muslim am I! I am this body, a play of five elements; a drama of the spirit dancing with joy and sorrow.*

Pt Sirju was proving to be the inspired leader that his people was looking for. His objective was to engage the community and inspire them to bigger things. The purpose behind the India Independence march was to arouse in his people the pride and enthusiasm inspired from accomplishments of the mother country.

Living with Purpose

Young Pt Sirju leading India Independence March

Rising Influence

Through Pt Sirju's hard work and peaceful and influential nature, he became other things to different people. He was the community peace-maker for families with any manner of disputes. Young couples facing family oppositions came to him for guidance and advice. As his popularity increased, so did also his list of chelas (god-children). These included people of all ages who wanted someone who could inspire and uplift them.

In those days, no one had telephones that they could call to make an appointment. On many occasions, after a day of community or priesthood work, he came home to find many individuals at his home, waiting for him to attend to their issues or requests. Some would leave to return another day, but most often they would continue to wait until he returned home.

Their needs varied from wanting to set a date for a religious function, bringing a sick child for him to pray over, checking patra

Beginnings of Spiritual Journey

(g), or finding a name for a newborn baby. Or, some needed spiritual guidance, marital counselling or to check out a gana (g). Upon his arrival home, he would always pleasantly greet them and start to offer his services even if he was tired and hungry. This would often continue late into the evening, but he was happy to serve as long as the person was willing to wait.

Pt Sirju's services were always free of charge and he never turned anyone away. He also never complained. Many people would start to arrive as early as 6 am with the idea of catching him before he left home, and he often let his breakfast get cold as he would leave his meal untouched if there was someone waiting to meet with him. His services were offered to all regardless of ethnicity, as many of the people of African descent from neighbouring Anns Grove, Bee Hive, Dochfour and Greenfield brought their sick babies for him to pray over.

Pt Sirju made it his duty to attend all funerals for members of the community. He claimed he was never too tired to go even though at times, it was obvious that he looked exhausted. He always made time to pray for the deceased. If through some unforeseen circumstances someone requested him at the last minute to perform funeral rites, as happened on many occasions, he was there.

Pt Sirju had presided at a funeral in addition to the many pujas he had performed on the last day of the Nowraat (g) period. Considered a sanctified period, there were always many scheduled pujas that he performed during this time. He arrived home very tired. Soon after, a gentleman from the nearby village of Hope Estate arrived to inform him that the priest who was scheduled to do his puja did not show up. Since the man had already made all preparations, he hoped Pt Sirju would assist him by going to his home to conduct the puja. It was 10:00 p.m. and Pt Sirju was tired, but he hopped on his bicycle and proceeded to the man's home.

Although Pt Sirju was now spending a major portion of his time serving the community, the senior members within the community were looking to him to become a full time priest. They needed their priest to not only serve the community's personal needs, but to take full ownership of all temple activities. Once again, he was persuaded by a few vocal members of the community led by Hanooman to add this role to his responsibilities. While assuming this responsibility, he continued performing his roles at the store, where he was responsible to purchase goods and take care of the accounting for the business.

In 1952, at 28 years old, Pt Sirju was elected Secretary and Pandit of Clonbrook Hindu Temple; a position that he was annually re-elected to for twenty eight years. Through his leadership, the temple was not only a place of worship, but it became a center of learning for children of all ages. He taught children to sing and also taught Hindi and courses on spirituality. He recruited volunteer teachers to offer different topics including music and drama. He created singing groups for children and youths to perform at various religious functions, and become engaged in the events. For the adults, he influenced the formation of Chowtal (g) and Ramayana groups. They celebrated the various religious and cultural events in colorful style.

Bhose Harripaul, his godson and a young boy at the time, remembers some of the activities in these words:

> *My Guru was a humble, simple, knowledgeable and spiritual person who had an enormous influence and impact on my life. As a young boy, I recall attending the Clonbrook Hindu temple where I was taught Hindi, obedience and other religious duties from him, something I cherish and continue to advance throughout my life. I grew fascinated with his depth of knowledge about Hinduism and other religions. His devotion and commitment to Hinduism allowed him to travel throughout the vast coastline of Guyana and later in life Trinidad and Canada, inspiring the lives of devotees with his knowledge. His teachings and encouragement to young children were remarkable, as he always made himself available for discussions about the Hindu religion and whatever adversity affected you, in spite of the demands of his family and personal life.*

Beginnings of Spiritual Journey

Harold Kowlessar, also a young boy at the time, describes how Pt Sirju was looked upon:

> *Functions at the mathya (g) were always impressive under his leadership. His attire always seemed whiter than most, neat and well pressed. While we as boys were more interested in how many 'bells' were gone to gauge when refreshments were to be served, Pandit Ji was always a figure deserving of respect and adoration.*

Through Pt Sirju's influence and dynamic leadership, the youths and young adults were channelled into activities and endeavours that promoted personal growth and social conscience. These areas included debating skills, scholarship, drama and community efforts.

Latchman Kissoon remembers the days with these words:

> *He became very popular and respected having united Hindus, Muslims and Christians in Clonbrook. Right at this time, Pt Sirju took on the mantle of the village priest, and the temple became crowded with youths and elders alike; such was the attraction and popularity of the young priest.*

Leading Yajnas

Pt Sirju's stars were lining up in perfect unison. The love he exuded for all peoples, irrespective of race or religion, was keenly felt in the way he conducted his life. No one was turned away if they showed up at his doorstep with a request, financial or otherwise. In return, his community loved him.

In the area of his skills as a preacher, he had become not only learned, but a dynamic public speaker as well. The talent was not lost on the people in the community. They planned many activities in order to get the most out of their newly emerged spiritual leader.

One of these activities was a yajna. A yajna is essentially a sacrifice to God, done under stringent conditions. The sacrifice required the principal participants to observe a disciplined schedule and lifestyle for the duration of the event which in those days, lasted about 7 days. There were 3 sessions per day: 9-12 noon; 1-3 p.m. and 7- 10 p.m. A vegetarian meal was served after each session. The meal was provided by voluntary communal efforts, and open to all races. The principal participants included the priest, pandavas (gl) and srotas (handful of people who were designated to sit together with pandavas).

According to the Hindu scriptures, to gain the full benefits of a yajna, one must embark on it with purity of body, mind and soul. Along with the strict diet, a quiet atmosphere is provided in order to help prepare the participants for the event. The location for the yajna was cleaned and decorated and the environment needed to be tranquil.

Pt Sirju encouraged all of the principal participants to stay in a secluded location where they would observe strict fasting. The priest and pandavas as a group stayed at one home in the village, while the srotas stayed at another home. For the entire 7 days, these participants moved only between the yajna and the home at which they were staying, with no other diversions. For these individuals, the yajna was a huge sacrifice as they maintained a diet that was salt, onion and garlic free, prepared by a designated group of individuals assigned as cooks for the specialised meals. The purpose for this specialised bland diet, was dictated by Lord Krishna in the Bhagavad Gita as 'sattvic' that is, food that promotes a pure and calm body, mind and spirit.

All preparations and activities related to the conduct of the yajna was done on a communal, voluntary effort. Major activities done ahead of time included the rice which needed to be sifted through to ensure it was cleaned, the achaar (g) needed to be made weeks before, and puri (g) required many person-efforts. The men would cut the wood to set up the tent as venue for the yajna, and they assisted in building a singhasan (g) for the Pandit to sit in. Then everyone would participate in decorating the site.

The entire event ran like clock-work. It was well organised, and each person knew what his/her responsibility was. For example, if there was heavy rainfall during one of the sessions, the boys who were assigned would drain the water out using poles. The general air of cooperation, optimism and festivity described the mood of the community during this period.

First Yajna

Dhori Raghunauth moved from Corentyne Village, Berbice, to Bee Hive in 1952. Dhori had quickly demonstrated leadership and organizational skills. He succeeded in getting the local municipality to make infrastructure improvements in the construction of better roads and bridges in the community. In 1953, the residents of Bee Hive planned to host a yajna with Dhori as the organizer and Pt Sirju as the officiating priest. Being new to the village and not yet acquainted with its people, Dhori at first balked at the idea of being the organiser. At the persuasions of Pt Sirju and Balmeek Kissoon, a prominent local businessman, he accepted the offer.

The year was 1953, Guyana (then British Guiana) was in a state of uprising and a curfew was in effect. The elections of that year had resulted in the Peoples Progressive Party (PPP) earning a majority of seats in the Legislature. This created a cause of concern for the British Government which feared communist influences in the British colony. Thus, they suspended the constitution, declared a state of emergency and placed the country under military occupation.

Under these conditions, permission to proceed with the yajna was required. Pt Sirju accompanied Dhori to the office of Commissioner of Police from whom they received the required permission. The yajna was performed on the dam bordering Clonbrook and Bee Hive.

It was Pt Sirju's first yajna, the subject was Lord Rama's exploits as portrayed in the holy Ramayana.

With his godfather Pt Ramphair Tiwari, a venerable and learned priest in the audience, Pt Sirju gave an inspiring rendition of the ancient scriptures. It inspired the people of Bee Hive to sponsor three more yajnas in quick succession, with Pt Sirju as the officiating pandit.

> *I recall many Yagnas that he officiated at and he was praised by all of his peers for his adroit delivery and wisdom.*
> — Harold Kowlessar

Fortitude

The country was in political turmoil, but the village was thriving in terms of cultural and social mobility, in great part due to the dedication of their spiritual leader and his equally dedicated group of committee members who supported and admired his endeavours.

In those days, walking was the easiest way to get to a destination, not that there were many other options. Pt Sirju often used a bicycle to move around within the hamlet. One day, he walked to conduct a puja in Hope Estate, three villages away. To reach his destination, he needed to pass through the village of Dochfour. When he arrived there, he found the village to be flooded. Onlookers who saw his dilemma expected to see him turn back, but instead he hiked up his dhoti and crossed the water to continue with his journey. The people looking on were surprised and impressed at his fortitude.

On another occasion, cycling to do a puja at Unity, two villages away, Pt Sirju's bicycle got a flat tire. Without any hesitation, he followed his instinct which was to push the bike and continue. Minor inconveniences such as this could not deter him in any way from whatever he set out to do.

Beginnings of Spiritual Journey

Cars were a luxury item and beyond the reach of most of the inhabitants in the Guyana countryside. However, this limitation did nothing to prevent people moving from place to place as needed. Whether by motorcycle, speed boat, or tractors, the people were resourceful in acquiring and adapting to the appropriate modes of travel. Pt Sirju was often the willing beneficiary to the use of these various ways of getting around and often looked on them as an adventure. As was a universal truth on his life, he was open to all the options. He did not setup artificial barriers - such as an unwillingness to hop on a motor cycle for instance - and instead took others along for the ride, physically, mentally and spiritually. Whether this was his kids, friends, or whoever happened to be close at hand.

As a young boy, his son Hemant accompanied Pt Sirju to many pujas across the country. Hemant described their travels using the several modes of transportation. When on occasion they got messy in the process, Pt Sirju never complained, irrespective of how muddied they got. On one occasion, they went to Highbury across the Berbice River to preside at a function for Bhawan Singh's family. Bhawan, Pt Sirju's close friend, travelled with them in the vehicle while Udal Singh, also a family friend, travelled alongside in another vehicle. The yajman came out with a tractor trailer to pick them up. It was raining heavily and the roads were littered with potholes as deep as two to three feet. The wheels of the tractor spun in the potholes and mud was splattered everywhere but it did not matter to Pt Sirju. They journeyed back by boat, and on arriving home his mother was shocked at the dried mud caked onto their clothing.

On a few occasions, Hemant accompanied his dad to Ogle on the East Coast Guyana where his dad was presiding over a function. Arriving by taxi at the public road in Ogle, they were taken on motorcycles by Pt Sirju's godsons along the cobbled road to their home. Once the function concluded, they were driven on the motorcycle to the public road to get a taxi home. On another occasion when Pt Sirju was to preside at a function in Champagne,

East Coast Demerara, they were taken over the river with a small engine boat.

However, Sirju's main means of transportation within the confines of the village hamlets was his bicycle. In addition to rising above the challenges of flat tires, and floods, there were other hazards associated with his bicycling. He was heading to a puja in a neighbouring village when the bicycle stopped moving after a while. He jumped off only to realize that the end of his dhoti was wrapped around the pedal. Life was never dull.

Comfort for the Community

Mrs. Jhawanti Ramnarain's first memory of Pt Sirju dates back to January 1948, when at age twenty four, he officiated at her wedding held at Number 2 Canal, on the West Coast, Demerara. It was the first wedding ceremony that he conducted.

She related that through all the years she had known him, she was struck with his generosity. At the end of any religious function where he officiated, he sought out the poor and elderly in the congregation to whom he distributed the aarti collection. In the days when the poor and elderly nowah lady Jugri prepared the site for the religious puja, she was always the first and sure beneficiary of such charity from Pt Sirju.

Mrs. Ramnarain described that as recently as 2009, soon after a fire destroyed his home in Markham Canada, Pt Sirju conducted a puja for a community member. At the end, as was his standard practice, he offered her (Mrs. Ramnarain) the aarti cash, insisting on her to accept it. She related that she told him that she could not accept, since his home had just been destroyed and he needed the cash more than she did. It was a trait that he showed during his entire life, to give away the dachna he received to the poor, young and those in need.

Beginnings of Spiritual Journey

Pt Sirju's son Shiv remembers often waiting for prasad (g) and other goodies from his father after he finished his pujas, only to discover that his father had given them away to the villagers, usually the black children. It was a rare treat for these children and Pt Sirju could provide for his son in other ways.

Pt Sirju's life's impact and the comfort and guidance he provided to those around him cannot be better expressed than through the words from one of his god children Basmattie Doobay. Basmattie Doobay and her siblings were in Enmore, Guyana in January, 2010 for their sister's funeral. Unknown to them, Pt Sirju coincidentally, was visiting Guyana at the same time. In her own words:

> *When Guru walked in at the funeral that day, you cannot imagine our emotion. It was like our own dad had walked in. All of my sisters and brothers and all of the grandchildren ran towards him, and even though the grandchildren did not know him, they had heard of him from us. All of us held on to him. It was like a comfort that was missing and our grief just lifted when he walked in. It was a sad, very hard day for us but it was also a good day because he was there.*

She would never forget that day. She said that the day after the funeral they had just returned from collecting the ashes, and he was already there to checkup on how they were coping. All of her seven siblings including herself were christened by Pt Sirju. He was the only priest, other than her father, the late Sunny Ramchandar, who was ever invited to conduct their family pujas. She said that whenever she phoned Pt Sirju and he was busy or napping, he never failed to return the call and would inquire about the well being of the family.

How was he able to project the charisma and healing to those around who were hurting? By using his favourite text, the Bhagavad Gita, he often found the solution to many problems or questions one could encounter. At any moment, he had many of these verses at his fingertips. He understood that he was only an instrument to convey the messages handed down from these scriptures. As Basmattie added, there was no conversation with Pt Sirju where he omitted quoting a Sanskrit verse from the Bhagavad Gita.

As Pt Sirju made it his duty to attend all wakes and funerals in the community to provide support to bereaved families, a much repeated refrain of his on the passing of a dear one, was the following Sanskrit quote from the Bhagavad Gita:

> *Nainam chindanti sastrani*
> *Nainam dahati pavakah*
> *Na caiman kledayanty apo*
> *No sosayati marutah*

> *The soul can not be cut by any weapon, nor can be burned by fire, water cannot wet it, wind cannot wither.*

Gangadei Hemraj and her husband were godchildren of Pt Sirju. Her husband had been ailing for some time, and Gangadei said that whenever she spoke to her godfather, her spirit lifted and she felt better. Her godfather would sing a few lines of a bhajan and translate the meaning of it to her in addition to quoting from the Ramayana and Gita. He was encouraging and comforting and he told her that she was blessed in being able to take care of her sick husband. Her godfather requested that they phone him at anytime that they needed someone to talk to.

Lakharam Jaipargas, another one of Pt Sirju's godsons, lived in Mahaica, about five miles east of Clonbrook. His family ran successful businesses in Guyana and Canada. Lakharam, now living in Toronto, said that at his mother's and father's desire, Pt Sirju became his Guru in 1955; some 58 years ago. The family was poor and struggling to make ends meet, but that changed right after he got christened by Pt Sirju. Their lives started to improve financially and he believes that it was all due to the blessings he received from his Guru.

Beginnings of Spiritual Journey

Walter Dipchand, a former police officer from the neighbouring village of Unity refers to Pt Sirju as, "that great icon, he was the greatest spiritual leader that I have ever associated with." Walter provided a variant on the theme on the humility and influence of Pt Sirju. The incident occurred at a funeral - another funeral. (At this point the reader is thinking that this Priest attended one too many funerals. The pattern elicited a humorous comment from his son Ravi after dropping Pt Sirju off to attend one such event in Toronto, "*I hope all these people will remember me when my time comes*"). Walter related that one of his relatives had passed away and Pt Sirju, shortly before migrating to Canada in the nineteen eighties, attended the funeral at Bush Lot, West Coast Berbice. Pt Sirju was not dressed in priest's attire, he was in regular shirt and pants, so he was not identifiable as a priest unless one knew him. The presiding priest announced that if anyone was qualified to speak, they were invited to go up to the podium. Walter was not impressed with the presiding priest's condescending tone in his supposition that an "unqualified" speaker might show up. Walter had spotted Pt Sirju in the audience, and as Pt Sirju had developed a reputation as a dynamic speaker, persuaded Pt Sirju to take the microphone. According to Walter, his hypnotic voice left the gathering mystified. This was the influence Pt Sirju had everywhere he went.

Vishnu Jagroo, a godson from the village of Bee Hive, recollected that when he was a young man, he traveled often among the various villages. Hearing that he was a resident of Clonbrook, the people he met wanted to know whether he knew Pt Sirju, and would then proceed to praise Pt Sirju highly. Vishnu attests that his god father had a heart of gold, and that he has not seen his godfather's qualities in any other human being, nor been inspired by anyone more than him.

The Jagnandan family of Clonbrook had this to say of Pt Sirju:

> *One of his ardent admirers, the late Justice Ramraj Jagnandan of Clonbrook, in his acceptance address as a*

Lawyer to the High Court in Guyana stated that Pt Sirju had a profound influence on his life, with his timely advice, encouragement and spiritual guidance.

The real work of the rest of Pt Sirju's lifetime had begun in earnest.

> *Live as if you were to die tomorrow. Learn as if you were to live forever.*
> – Mahatma Gandhi

Beginnings of Spiritual Journey

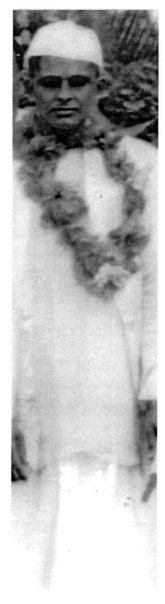

Pt Sirju in his 30's after a puja in the Clonbrook temple ground

CHAPTER 6

The Rising Priest (Mathya Transformation and 7 Day Yajna)

When one knows thee, then alien there is none, then no door is shut. Oh, grant me my prayer that I may never lose the bliss of the touch of the one in the play of many.
— Rabindranath Tagore

Mud Mathya

Pt Sirju was habitually attuned to every potential source of inspiration that could benefit both himself and the community.

In 1951, a visitor from India, Swami (g) Avaitanandaji Maharaj, toured the country on a mission to revive the teachings of Hinduism. Pt Sirju and temple members invited the world renowned spiritual leader to visit their village of Clonbrook. Swami Avaitanandaji accepted the invitation and preached and lectured for seven days. He covered a wide range of topics on Hinduism and their connection to daily life. At the end of his lecture series, the Swami drew the attention of the village residents to a subject of distress for him. He stated to the large gathering that he was impressed with the beautiful homes in the village. He remarked that the people were hardworking and, judging from the fact that they invited him to speak to them, they wanted to improve their quality of life. Then he asked, how were they content to worship in a building that seemed so out of place against the more progressive background of their modern homes?

The Swami gestured at the mud mathya structure being used to conduct regular worship. Up until now, the structure had served the needs of the people. Located in a fairly large plot of land, it was constructed of wooden walls and zinc roofing with a mud floor. Sonarin, a kindly old lady, lived across the temple grounds. Her name meant wife of goldsmith, a name that stuck even after her husband passed away. Popularised in the village for her trademark mouth-watering mitthais (g), she was also known for a quiet fastidiousness. This extended to the regular daubing (g) that she gave to the humble mud interiors of the mathya, which gave the floors a perpetual pristine look.

The origins to the mathya and the land on which it stood dated back to around 1923. This was when a group of the early settlers in the village started to look for a place to conduct religious services. The group consisted of Jugun - father of Harriram, Ramsamuj, Mahabir Maraj and Gopaul's nana. The group approached their local council representative Raghunandan Senior with a request for approval to build a Hindu temple on a plot of land that extended from the middle walk (g). Raghunandan Senior was able to obtain the required permission from the District Commissioner, following which the group prepared and built the land. The first Hindu temple in the village, built from coconut branches, was completed around the same year. Around 1940's, this structure was replaced by the mud mandir. However, the question of the land ownership still persisted.

Living with Purpose

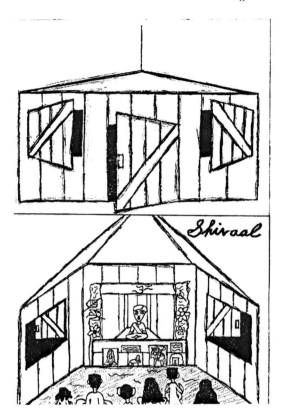

Mud Mathya

Some of the villagers who attended the mathya as children looked back with nostalgia on their recollection of the antique edifice, simple and unassuming. They argued that it would have been wise to have saved the relic as a memorial to life in the good old days. Life imitates art, the nostalgia is no doubt linked to a desire to return to the days when life was much simpler.

The swami had an opposing view. What he saw was an artifact that was incongruous with the changes he saw around him. The mathya stuck out as a sore thumb to the visitor.

Pt Sirju agreed with the swami, but he was well aware of the economic situation of the villagers. He knew that they did not have the resources to fund a new temple. He also knew that some of them

The Rising Priest (Mathya Transformation and 7 Day Yajna)

were fond of the mathya as it was, and may not trust outsiders to direct, design or build something bolder or ostentatious.

Pt Sirju rose from the congregation to respond to the question the Swami posed to the audience. He explained that first of all, in order to construct a new edifice, they would need permission from the village council for continued use of the land for the said purpose. He stated that if Raghunandan Senior, who happened to be in the audience, would help resolve the issue by providing the necessary approvals, him (Pt Sirju) and the residents of the village would work together to replace the mud temple with a proper temple building.

At this proposal, and before the council representative could respond, many in the audience stood up in succession to show their support. Everyone promised that if they received approval for use of the land, they would join with Pt Sirju to provide the financial and material support needed to construct the new temple. At the show of solidarity, Raghunanan got to his feet and announced that he would obtain the necessary approvals.

An ad hoc committee, initially consisting of twenty seven members, was formed to manage a project to rebuild the temple. The challenges were many, not the least of which was obtaining the required funds. Cash was scarce and its availability within the local communities was very limited. Over and above his other duties, Pt Sirju took on the task to lead the committee's efforts in collection of finances and materials towards building and painting the temple. To collect funds for the new temple project meant that the committee members needed to go house to house. Because of limited cash within the community, the committee members would sometimes experience verbal abuse in the process of trying to collect the funds. Pt Sirju because of his prominence as a Hindu priest, was in the forefront to solicit the funds. Through his singular influence, successful business people across the country provided generous contributions in cash and other resources towards the project. He was focused in working to elevate his community, and the efforts and success in this endeavour once again confirmed his leadership ability.

Other challenges included the diverse opinions and expectations for the project within the project team, not an unexpected state of affairs considering the large number of members that made up the group. As a result, many members dropped off during the unexpectedly long eight years it took to complete the project. But Sirju and a handful of members stuck to the task at hand. These members included: Manoo, Mathura, Dhori Raghunauth, Jagoo, Bhawan Singh, Hanooman, Jack Jagnandan, the senior Raghunandan, Seenanan, and Jai Hoolas among a few others whose names have now been lost in the annals of the collective village memory.

Dhori Raghunauth was one of the few residents of the community who outlived Pt Sirju. He passed away at the ripe age of ninety two in October 2013. Just days before his own passing, he related that it was not easy in those early days to manage the temple and its activities, and at the same time manage projects.

The statistics coming out of construction of the new temple bear to some of the difficulties that Dhori Raghunauth refer. The project started with twenty seven members, and took eight years to complete. It ended with a lot fewer members, many of them came on board at later stages during the project. As Thakur Persaud a former resident explained, *many members were replaced, others left in frustration because of internal squabbles and disagreements among members. Pt Sirju and a few staunch members stuck manfully to their task.*

Pt Sirju, who was soft spoken, could not win over all of his members. He did however receive full cooperation from those who stayed on purpose with him in completing the project. Many members left due to the time the projects and temple activities required. Dalia recalls that Pt Sirju seldom had any free time of his own. Whenever he was not administering temple activities including preparing reports in his role as secretary, raising funds, or doing pujas, he would eke time for his family. His devotion kept him incredibly busy, but it also fulfilled him.

First 7 Day Yajna

R.S. Singh, the owner of RSSingh Lumber Ltd. was one of the wealthy individuals who donated large sums towards the project. Singh had originally planned on sponsoring a yajna in his native township of Anna Catherina, but later decided that the most suitable occasion, venue and pandit would be the temple opening in the village of Clonbrook, presided over by Pt Sirju. He had full confidence and faith in its people. He only needed to convince his family members, all of whom hailed from the district of Anna Catherina, and naturally would have preferred to celebrate the family successes with a yajna in their own home town. Seeing the love and collaboration of the people of Clonbrook and their leader Pt Sirju, Singh's family members were easily convinced that this was the right setting for the yajna.

The considerable financial support that he provided resulted in the eventual completion of the construction of the temple including the painting. Through their close collaboration over the years on the temple project, Singh had come to know Pt Sirju very well and was impressed with his dedication. Through the working relationship with Pt Sirju, he also came to know the strong group of committed and informed individuals that stood behind him. This group of dedicated individuals would go to any length to promote the interest of the community and the dharma (g).

In 1959 the new temple was finally completed in Clonbrook. RS Singh provided all the funds needed to commemorate the opening in grand style. The event would take the form of a 7 day yajna, and would be the first 7 day yajna that Pt Sirju presided over. Singh's wife, his mother, and his aunt were among the residents who sat as *srotas* to listen to the yajna.

The yajna was another major personal test for the young Pt Sirju. There were a few first metaphorical hurdles in terms of proving his ability at the podium. Although he had presided at four previous yajnas, this one was different in many ways. It was the first time he was presiding over a 7 day event and with 3 sessions each day, he needed to be well prepared. There would be knowledgeable and experienced pandits in the audience, as well as the youths of the community who were questioning their faith and would be looking to Pt Sirju for inspiration.

Moreover, he needed to convince each member of the community that he was fully capable to be a full time pandit, who could manage the new temple and still be able to fully serve the community. A successful performance was needed to quell any existing doubts on his readiness and capabilities.

As politics have a role in most situations requiring some diplomacy, Dalia, the quiet lady behind Pt Sirju's more public persona, sensed a need to circumvent any potentially negative fallouts from her husband's novel performance. She encouraged him to ask his mentor, the learned and experienced Pt Ramsahai Doobay, to attend the opening. The presence of his mentor, she urged, would not only provide the young priest with advice and support, but would serve to allay any doubts or criticisms from potential detractors on the young priest's performance. Here one senses the strong subtle force behind Pt Sirju's successes and why he and his dharampatni (g) made a great team! The Dalia-Pt Sirju team remained strong for 65 years. Their sixty-fifth wedding anniversary occurred one month after Pt Sirju's passing.

Pt Ramsahai Doobay attended the opening and was satisfied with the performance of his protégé. The only criticism he provided was the casual style in which Pt Sirju wrapped his pagri, a skill he never really excelled in!

Pt Sirju also enjoyed the presence of his god father, Pt Ramphair Tiwari, who was at his side for the entire duration of the yajna. The latter was also a learned and well respected Hindu priest in Guyana. His presence during the entire event provided much support and encouragement, as well as invaluable feedback to the young priest.

The Rising Priest (Mathya Transformation and 7 Day Yajna)

Jhawanti Ramnarain recalled that he looked majestic when he sat on the singhasan reading yajnas and how beautifully he read and chanted.

The yajna and its successful conclusion marked another major milestone in the life of Pt Sirju. With the opening of the new temple, he was chosen by the temple committee as official temple priest. Responsible for all affairs relating to temple activities, he conducted all services which included regular Sunday services, as well as the celebration of all religious events such as Ram Nawmi, Janam Ashtmi, etc. The temple committee was so impressed with him that they initiated a rule that he should be the only priest allowed to sit on the singhasan in the temple.

The qualities he possessed prompting singular devotion from committee members could perhaps be summarised by the words of the Jagnandan family:

> *As a Priest in Clonbrook and neighbouring villages, he was well admired and respected. His personality was a harmonious blend of a Priest, Teacher, Advisor as well as a Father. His warm approaching smile, simplicity, impeccable honesty and integrity, and devotion to the principle of Sanatan Dharma (g) were all unquestionable.*

These were the days before telephones in the countryside. Whenever there was a yajna in his village, Pt Sirju would travel many miles to extend invitations to priests and singers of the different communities. On many instances they wouldn't be at home or he couldn't find them, therefore he would make several trips to extend his personal invitations. He went to great lengths to make sure everyone was given a chance to attend. His insights about the glorious Hindu scriptures, delivered in his beautiful melodious voice, became very popular throughout the Guyana countryside.

Temple Activities and Duties

A large family did nothing to detract Pt Sirju from fulfilling his mission as a full-time priest and philanthropist. Temple operations, priestly duties and collecting funds for various projects such as temple improvements took up much of his time. He received total support and encouragement from the team of village stalwarts who formed the initial Temple Committee, and who elected him as their leader. These stalwarts included Raghunandan Senior who served as President of the Committee for fifteen years, later followed by Seelall, then Bhawan Singh. Other members of the team included Manoo, Mathura, Dhori Raghunauth, Jagoo, Hanooman, Jack Jagnandan, Lilya and other prominent villagers.

Pt Sirju was an untiring leader at the forefront of his team working on many enterprises. As temple priest, he spent a large portion of his time on temple activities. Under this mantle, one of the roles he assumed was that of Secretary to the Clonbrook Hindu Temple Committee. In this position, he was responsible to organise monthly meetings, get quorums, and conduct the meetings. Following the conclusion of the meeting, he documented and distributed minutes and followed up with members by personally delivering the minutes to their homes.

The carbon paper he used to write minutes and summons for the temple meetings now seem archaic, and a medium of days long gone by. The content for summons were only a few lines, as its purpose was to inform the committee members of the date of the next meeting. To optimise and save paper, he folded the long sheet of carbon paper and stripped it into widths to just accommodate each summon. The end result was that he got the maximum number of summons, as well as a record of who it was made out to. He was an excellent record keeper.

There were no telephones or social media such as emails or Facebook in those days. But, being gregarious, he likely enjoyed the opportunity to visit with the members for a nice conversation while he delivered his notes and minutes! Later, his children helped with the delivery or, someone was always around to hand deliver these notes. Someone such as Pollo. Dependable and gregarious, Pollo relished the little assignments of delivering notes and minutes. It gave him a sense of fulfilment and, being opinionated, he had no qualms in voicing his opinions on community happenings to those he met, spoken out loud with no shade of subtlety or blandishment.

Pollo had been born a normal baby. However a few months after birth, the baby suffered epileptic fits, after which his eyes remained curled upward. As he grew older, he gradually lost more of his vision. However, he was a hardworking individual, and was always willing to lend a helping hand whenever someone needed it, whether as a farm labourer or a courier of information.

Pollo was popular in the village. He was everywhere to be seen and had a few favourite homes where he would visit whenever he needed a meal. Most of the people were delighted to help him. Some ridiculed him as being dim-witted because of his physical appearance, but others knew that he was a clever individual, very much aware of what was going on around him.

One of Pollo's favorite homes to visit was Pt Sirju's, where there would be kind words offered or a meal ready. Pt Sirju's daughter Basso always had something that she would quickly fix up for Pollo to eat when he showed up unexpectedly. Pt Sirju took him along to any puja or ceremonies, for he was a good and lively companion. At the same time, Pollo loved the outing and the entertainment and refreshments that followed. Not surprisingly, he was doggedly loyal to Pt Sirju and his family.

Pollo regularly accompanied Pt Sirju to the temple committee meetings. Here, he loved listening in to temple discussions. He was sensitive to the different points of view going on around him and sat quietly in the background, taking in the debates among the members. As they were leaving to go home after one of these meetings, Pollo mentioned to Pt Sirju that he hadn't had anything to eat all day. Pt Sirju took him to his home and checked in his kitchen where he was able to find some food to appease the hunger of his friend.

The discussions of the committee usually kept the meeting going until midnight. These discussions and planning covered all matters that touched on life in the community and outside of it. Not only those that related to the spiritual aspects of life, but to the social, intellectual and economic as well. Items such as: plans for the next celebration; assessing the health of the community (what social issues need to be addressed; who needed assistance and of what nature); what educational courses were needed for the different age groups; how to find teachers for each subject; what classical activities—drama, debating, or choir—should they offer to the youth; what opportunities existed outside the community walls to expand the horizons of its members; and how could they help others outside of the community.

On a more mundane level, the committee also managed resources such as utensils and large pots which were available to be lent to the community for occasions such as weddings. Also, managing day to day temple operations such as cleaning, washing sheets, and shining lotas (g) etc. needed to be taken care of. The committee was involved in each aspect of the proper maintenance of the temple.

Community and temple activities remained a consummate preoccupation in Pt Sirju's day to day life. As he and the temple committee members identified areas for improvement within the community, Pt Sirju was also never at a loss to arrive at creative ways to solve issues.

In the mid sixties, the temple needed funds for ongoing maintenance and restoration work. In the older days, he and the temple committee members would resort to door to door canvassing to collect funds. This time, he came up with a brighter idea.

He solicited the help of his younger brother, Hansraj. With Hansraj at his side helping to plan and organise the event, he produced a show meant to not only entertain but to be culturally uplifting for the residents. It featured classical music and dance items. A popular local singer, Tillack, played the saxophone and he was accompanied by a classical dancer.

Despite the elaborate planning and preparations, only a few people that included close associates from temple committee, attended the event. The small audience was appreciative of the talented artists and enjoyed the event, but the show was a financial failure.

As a lover of music and dance, it was logical that Pt Sirju chose this medium as a means to raise funds. However, the village during these times was still a mainly closeted community. The notion of associating dance forms with religion seemed an alien concept for the people of this small community. There was some difficulty understanding that classical dancing had been in practice by Hindus for the longest time. The art was a long ago practice in ancient India, and legendary in Hindu mythology. More recently, classical dancing is readily accepted in the temples for fundraising and other cultural and religious events. But at the time, Pt Sirju's vision was way ahead of the crowd. The episode was one more example of his progressive and innovative mindset, an overarching characteristic of his leadership style.

> *Two roads diverged in a wood and I - I took the one less traveled by, and that has made all the difference.*
> – Robert Frost

Working with Youth

Pt Sirju was leader, teacher, coach, mentor, friend and priest. This called for being both a leader and follower. He himself taught courses such as Hindi and singing. This transitioned into creation of kirtan (g) groups for the youths and children as a way to engage them and the congregations in the ceremonies. In addition to bhajans, the groups were taught chowtal and ramayan by Dwarkanauth, a dedicated temple patron. Pt Sirju enjoyed the two types of singing and would join in the singing whenever he could.

Basmatie (Prandai) Singh belonged to the first batch of youngsters who attended all temple activities at the time when Pt Sirju became the temple priest. She recalled that Pt Sirju trained her, Liloutie (Leila) Ramsaywack – another young woman, and Raj - Pt Sirju's daughter, to sing bhajans. They often accompanied Pt Sirju to many pujas where they sang the bhajans he taught. As they accompanied him to these pujas, they complained when they had to walk long distances to get to the destination. He was a demanding taskmaster, insisting that they continue walking, as the distance was short, for he believed it was important to impress on the importance of offering prayers through the pujas; and that it was an honor to be given the opportunity.

Leila was a student of Pt Sirju at the temple since she was about eleven years old. She remembered the numerous religious discussions he had with her and the other young students. She still recalls how he never got angry with anyone and she never saw a flaw in him. From since that age, she felt that he excelled as a teacher and preacher. She was struck by his love for humanity.

Leila accompanied Pt Sirju to the many pujas and yajnas he performed. She stated that Pt Sirju took the choir group to all the religious functions in the village and would pick them up if they needed to go to other villages. He encouraged her to grow her skills in public speaking by writing short speeches from the religious texts such as the Ramayana for her to present. He encouraged her to learn the speeches so that she could do the presentation without referring to her notes. He also taught her to sing and would write chowpaees (g) and little stories for her to sing and read. She stated that through his teachings, she knew all the little prayers. She felt that he had completed his mission of encouraging young children in public speaking and in recognising the importance and power of prayers.

Prandai also credits Pt Sirju for teaching her all the bhajans and prayers that she knows. As he did with Leila, Pt Sirju wrote speeches

The Rising Priest (Mathya Transformation and 7 Day Yajna)

and gave them to her to present in addition to teaching her to sing bhajans. He motivated everyone to reach their full potential and was thrilled when they did not need to refer to their notes because they remembered all of their speeches.

Prandai was noted for her beautiful singing voice as well. Her husband Balroop Singh was ailing with a serious heart condition. He requested his wife to tape a bhajan to be played at his funeral, as he knew that it would be difficult for her to sing it on that day. He passed away four days later and Prandai did not have enough time to tape the hymn. She mentioned to Pt Sirju about her late husband's wish. He encouraged her to sing the bhajan her husband requested, and assured her that he would help her fulfill her husband's desire. Spurred by Pt Sirju's encouragement, Prandai sang one of the bhajans Pt Sirju taught her at her husband's funeral. She stressed that Pt Sirju always encouraged her and all his students to grow, and do what's right.

Ravendra Kowlessar, who at that time was President of the Clonbrook Hindu Youth Organization (CHYO), remarked on the high esteem with which Pt Sirju's name was held especially in the Guyana countryside. Ravendra and his kirtan group had participated at a yajna in Mahaica, a village about five miles from Clonbrook. At the end of the group's presentation of bhajans, accompanied by their harmonium, drum and tabla performers, the master of ceremonies remarked that they were well trained by Pt Sirju.

Pt Sirju received praise wherever they performed. Ravendra remarked that Pt Sirju was so benevolent and well respected that no one turned them away when they were soliciting donations for the temple and events. All they had to do was mention his name.

Chantamonie Minkoo was a resident of the village who lived a few blocks away from Pt Sirju. He remembered the time when there was a friendly chowtaal singing competition between the Mahaica Creek Ramayana goal (g) and the Clonbrook team that included Pt Sirju. Chantamonie said of him: *He was a man of great morals, he not only gave advice to his devotees (g) but would sit and have discussions* with them after he was finished with their pujas. He practised what he preached. He also attended other ceremonies even when he was not presiding.

Ravenda Kowlessar said that while Pt Sirju taught Hindi at the temple, he recalled that he also taught at his home. Ravendra and his two brothers Apti and Gupti went to learn Hindi at the temple. He remembered one occasion during Pt Sirju's class when he and his friend were not paying attention. The object of their attention was a wiry dog coming down the street. While it was not unusual to see a dog, or for that matter a cat, donkey or goat sauntering idly along on the road at any time, as young kids (especially in a group) always looking for any distractions from the tedium of learning a strange language, the dog provided a welcome source of amusement. Being one who easily saw humour in situations, their teacher likely understood their easy absorption in the stray dog. However, he took his charge seriously – his focus was to tutor young minds - and by quickly calling attention to their momentary distraction, he brought them back to the class studies.

Pt Sirju's leadership fostered a culture of stimulating the youths to excel in all areas. It was a culture where members of the community who were trained or gifted with special talents were engaged to use their skills to contribute in special ways. An example of the artistry that came out of a highly energised collaboration was the production of '*Krishna Leela*' by members of the CHYO. The show depicted a collection of tales of Krishna's (g) antics performed while he was still a child below the age of ten.

One scene depicted the legend of Putana, the killer of infants who was sent by Krishna's evil uncle Kans to kill his baby nephew. Putana disguised as a cowherd entered Krishna's home and with his mother's permission, started to feed the infant her breast milk which contained poison. Although Krishna was only a baby, he already possessed divine powers, so he was not deceived by Putana's appearance. He immediately recognised her disguise and suckled so hard that the life was extracted from her body. Just before dying, she reverted to her original demonic form.

The play was written by teacher Jaikarran Seenanan and coordinated by Hansraj Raghunandan, a long time patron of the temple. The play was replete with drama and songs, one of the most endearing of which was the Lord Krishna bhajan, *Suna suna laage*. Translated, one of the paragraphs states: *Their love and affection for Him is beyond bounds. He has endeared Himself with all in the community. A friend to the young and beautiful, member of the family. The Charmer on the flute, and the Splendor of the cowherds yet, today He leaves for Mathura, breaking the hearts of all.*

The play was performed at many venues throughout the countryside such as Enmore and Industry. In the city of Georgetown, it was performed at Queens College, the top boys school of the time. All the actors knew their scripts and performed their roles to perfection. Response to the play was overwhelming. It was excellently coordinated and unique as the first of its kind produced in the country.

The quality and style of the productions reflected on how far the community and its ideals had risen. Pt Sirju had not only been instrumental in his own personal transformation, he inspired those around him to do the same. Thakur Persaud summed it up with the reflection.... *Not only had Pt Sirju undergone a personal transition but he also succeeded in transforming the entire Hindu community of Clonbrook and Bee Hive.*

The CHYO group felt so indebted to Pt Sirju that even when he moved to Canada, one of the members, Hansraj Raghunandan, suggested that they must keep him abreast of all that was happening in the village and send him an invitation for any functions.

Nandram Kissoon, from the Kissoon family in nearby Bee Hive, and now a retired Judge living in Guyana, related that Pt Sirju was responsible for bringing him and his brothers into the fold of the Hindu religion. He described the period during his youth when a missionary, Reverend Cropper, arrived in the village from India, with the purpose of converting the Hindus to Christianity. There was a prevailing condition at the time in British Guiana, requiring individuals to convert to Christianity in order to be considered suitable for teaching, some civil service (Government), and other professional positions. The Reverend, a Caucasian, spoke fluent Hindi, an asset where many of the first settlers in the village spoke only Hindi. Nandram's aja Sri Kissoon, and his father Harripersaud were both Hindus, but the Reverend was a close friend of Sri Kissoon. As a result, Harripersaud agreed to have Reverend Cropper conduct Christian services in his yard. The family viewed the Reverend's services as an opportunity to learn more about Christianity and as a venue for the villagers to socialise.

It was during this time that Pt Sirju came into the priesthood. His advent into the priesthood filled the dearth in Hindu leadership and influences in the community.

Pt Sirju spoke to the Kissoon family and advised them of the activities of the youth group at the Clonbrook Hindu temple and encouraged the young Kissoon boys to attend. And soon enough, the Kissoon brothers became proteges of Pt Sirju as well.

In addition to regular discussions on topics in the Hindu faith, Pt Sirju encouraged and inspired the boys to make presentations especially on the occasions of Hindu auspicious days. He would assist the two brothers Nandram and Latchman with sketches of stories from Hindu texts. To get the boys into the spirit of the occasion, he encouraged them to dress in the traditional dhoti whenever they addressed audiences at the mandir, and would assist in the somewhat intricate wrapping of their dhoti attire.

Nandram stated that Pt Sirju introduced them to the profound philosophies of the Hindu religion, which in turn made him and his brothers "non convertible". He attributed their staunch faith in the Sanatan Dharma religion to the education and insights that they received from Pt Sirju.

Nandram's brother Latchman, himself now a Pandit, and one of the Kissoon youths at the time of Pt Sirju's early priesthood wrote:

The Rising Priest (Mathya Transformation and 7 Day Yajna)

> *Panditji loved a microphone. He told his congregation that both Mahatma Gandhi and Pandit Nehru were barristers-at-Law of the inner temple in London, England and used examples such as these to inspire and encourage the youths to study. Through his persuasion the village of Clonbrook produced 6 Hindu lawyers two of whom became High Court Judges.*
>
> *He was a Guru to many, helping them in their quest for enlightenment.*
>
> *He had a tremendous influence on the Kissoon family who alone produced 5 lawyers. Many other families in the village produced scholars of international renown, among these scholars were those who attended his temple.*
>
> – Pt Dr Latchman P. Kissoon JP

Another youth that Pt Sirju influenced was Deodat Tiwari. Deodat credits Pt Sirju for setting him on a career path that has extended over his entire working life. He started on this path in 1971. In that year, he completed a program through which he qualified as a health inspector in Guyana. As he started to look for available positions in his field, there was one specific position that drew his attention. It had all the features that he was hoping for – it would utilise all his skills and it presented opportunities for growth and travel, which he enjoyed. He was elated when called for an interview. However, after waiting for feedback and not receiving any after many days had elapsed, he visited Pt Sirju. He regarded Pt Sirju as a trusted confidante and advisor, one with whom he could share his anxieties regarding plans for his future, and be certain to receive some clarity. He discovered that the latter through the conduct of his insurance work, was acquainted with the prospective employer. Pt Sirju met the employer and discussed his nephew's intense interest and suitability for the position and within a week, Deodat was hired. In 2014, the year that this book was written, Deodat was still employed in the same field in the United States. Deodat stated that Pt Sirju was a great man and that he never met a man with his qualities and pleasant personality.

People of Unity

His relationship with the people of the neighbouring Unity village went beyond that of priest and parishioners. Inasmuch as many of his god-children also came from Unity, there was a closeness and feeling of mutual love and admiration. When in Unity, he would visit each home that he went by, to enquire of the well being of family members, offer a prayer, or just to enjoy a quiet conversation and share a laugh. Never one to miss an opportunity for serious discourse, he was a regular visitor to the resident priest of Unity, Pandit Jaimangal, for lengthy discussions on the scriptures.

Some of his chelas in Unity included, Pt Sukhdeo Maharaj, Mrs Oloo, Seenanan and family, Buddy Boy, Paisoo, and others, among them Chandroutie Jagdeo, the mother of Guyana's ex president Bharat Jagdeo. His chelas would insist on loading him up with their freshly picked fruits and vegetables of all descriptions, as Unity was well known for its prolific agricultural accomplishments. In addition to agricultural successes, Unity produced educators, politicians and cricketers such as Shivnarine Chanderpaul. Doodnauth Hetram, was an example of a high profile educator who became Principal of Queens College. At the time, the college was Guyana's highest institution of learning for boys. Bharrat Jagdeo also from Unity, became President of Guyana during the late nineteen hundreds.

A few of the interactions with the people from this community is described in the remainder of this chapter.

Ramrattie Mohamaid, a resident of Unity, said that after listening to Pt Sirju officiate at a yajna in the early nineteen fifties, she wanted to be christened to him. She asked her mother to approach Pt Sirju on her behalf, and together with three of her sisters, they were christened by Pt Sirju. Shortly after their christening, there was a seven day, three session daily yajna in the Clonbrook temple yard. Ramrattie woke up each day at 5.00 am, dressed her two daughters for school, and began the morning trek from Unity to Clonbrook. They left home at 7.00 am, walked through the line dam stretch arriving in Clonbrook by 8.30 am.

She did not miss any sessions as she found her Guru's readings very uplifting. Each day, she garlanded him with a mala (g) that she made from freshly picked madaar (g) flowers, a sign of great respect and affection. At the end of the evening session, as they walked the three miles home, she and her companions were already excitedly looking forward to the next day's sessions.

Sukhdeo, a resident of Unity and patron of the Unity temple, described that children would surround Pt Sirju whenever he went to Unity to read a Yajna. Observing that the children usually arrived at the puja without greeting anyone, Pt Sirju used the opportunity as a teaching moment. Demonstrating with hands clasped, and saying *Seeta Ram,* after about the third session of the seven day yajna, the children were practising the greeting he taught. Pt Sirju influenced the children of Unity as a whole as well as mentored several students individually.

Pt Sirju also mentored Sukhdeo, whom he met while performing funeral rites for Mahabir, a gentleman from Unity. While at the cemetery, he learned that Sukhdeo, a grandchild of the deceased, was training to become a Pandit. Pt Sirju requested to be directed to the grandchild. He then approached the young man with encouraging words, and with an offer to help with his training. He invited him to visit his home, promising to provide guidance in his preparation to become a Pandit.

Sukhdeo visited Clonbrook village often to spend many days and nights at Pt Sirju's home. He was soon after christened by Pt Sirju. While visiting, he accompanied Pt Sirju to any puja, funeral, or other religious event that occurred during that time. The alliance took them to many villages, some as far as Mahaicony, about ten miles away. During the learning process, Pt Sirju would let Sukhdeo conduct the havan (g) ceremony and sing bhajans. After some time, once Pt Sirju was satisfied with the progress of his protégé, he started to recommend him as a Pandit to people in the community.

The period marked the beginning of a very close Guru - godson relationship. Pt Sukhdeo remarked that Pt Sirju never raised his voice at him when he made an error. Instead his guru would choose a moment when they were alone together and quietly review the occurrence. Pt Sirju would assist his protégé in clarifying any questions he had and Pt Sukhdeo would apologize and assure his mentor that he had learnt from the review. Both guru and godchild were utmost humble individuals.

In the year 1960, at thirty seven years, Pt Sirju performed a Bhagavat yajna at Unity, sponsored by people of this community.

Dr B. N. Kumar attended the yajna and these are his recollections:

> *I am very honored, tickled, and humbled to write on behalf of our dear and beloved Priest Sirju P. Misir. When I was asked to do this, by his son Pandit Jaiwant, I felt I must take this opportunity as Panditji was a noble, loving, and kind-hearted human being. Panditji was well-known, not only in Clonbrook, but also throughout the length and breadth of Guyana. Panditji has left a great legacy. One that is full of love for mankind, peace and reconciliation, and moreover, for family. The climax of one of his great and noble achievements was a yajna which he read at the Unity – Lancaster Hindu Temple. The temple was built on the land that my grandfather donated.*
>
> *I recall the occasion of the yajna vividly; it was well thought out, planned, managed, and executed. The yajna commenced with Sirju P. Misir on the singhasan. I remembered he was a tall and stately figure and by virtue of his demeanor, character, and personal deportment, he was able to gain the honor, dignity, and respect of all who attended and participated in the yajna. Panditji was well*

The Rising Priest (Mathya Transformation and 7 Day Yajna)

versed in the Ramayana, Gita, Upanishads, and the Vedas, the fountain of all knowledge as handed down from God to the four Rishis. Something that still resonates in my mind to this day is his intoned voice, sweet speech, and calmness, and the Godliness within him. As a matter of fact, I remember vividly, the lines of the bhajan ... Bhagwat Bhagwan Ke ... and even to this day, I sing that line sometimes. People will leave the yajna humming those lines. Everyday and night, he left lessons for his devotees, much of these lessons cut across the board, appealing to young people, adolescents, families, and the elderly. So, everyday, there were lessons to be learned and to be carried over. He believed in Education, for with a good education, there is power.

During the night sessions, cars would line up on either side of the public road, and filling up the cricket grounds nearby. People came from as far as from the cities of Rosignol and Georgetown because each night, he had a profound message for all his devotees. To go along with his readings, were songsters, drummers, Kirtan groups, and Hindi school children from various villages near and far. A popular singing, Taan singing, also took place. The readings lasted as late as 10:30 to 11:00 at night. Meals were served throughout the day and at night. Everyone was served with Prasad, such was the scenario of the noble and humble Priest, presiding over a one week yajna, at the small village of Unity.

Panditji engaged his audience. Questions were asked and discussed and people were always eager to listen and get the words of wisdom which came from his lips. Panditji was a profound scholar of Satya Sanatan Dharma. He made a vivid impression on thousands, not only during the yajna week, but also throughout his lifetime. Many fell to his feet in holy reverence as their Guru, and many were blessed over the weeks and years that he presided over the different functions, including the sanskars. Such was the trust and faith they had in Panditji.

Living with Purpose

Many young priests sat at his feet to get the fountain of knowledge from him. He was undoubtedly a humble teacher, a contemporary scholar in no uncertain terms, a simple human being with a smile that would make you feel good. His tone of voice was always soft and soothing and would appeal to anyone – rich or poor, big or small, or for a matter of fact, to anyone. Yes indeed, his overall personality would catch on you and make an impression on you even if you met him for the very first time.

This wonderful human being spent a full life on Earth, with his family, his congregation, and with the many young Priests he had trained so that they can carry out the work of Hindu Dharma. His legacy is one of forgiveness, love, compassion, empowerment, family, peace, and above all, his love for all mankind irrespective of religious beliefs, religious denominations, and cultures. He always sang a popular bhajan that was a favorite of Mahatma Gandhi. This is it:

Raghupati Raghav Raja Ram
Patita Pavan Sitaram
Sitaram, Sitaram
Bhaj Pyare Mana Sitaram
Raghupati Raghav Raja Ram
Patita Pavan Sitaram
Ishwar Allah Tero Nam
Sabko Sanmati De Bhagwan
Raghupati Raghav Raja Ram
Patita Pavan Sitaram
Mukhmen Tulsi Ghatamen Ram
Jab Bolo Tab Sitaram
Raghupati Raghav Raja Ram
Patita Pavan Sitaram

Over his lifetime, he schooled many youngsters and mended many broken minds and homes.

May his soul rest in peace and may he shower his many blessings on this family, friends, and all those with whom he has been in contact.
God Bless.

Dr. B. N. Kumar
Professor NYIT;Research Fellow
Columbia University;
Professor Dowling College Doctoral Students

You have to grow from the inside out. None can teach you, none can make you spiritual. There is no other teacher but your own soul.

— Swami Vivekananda

Young Pt Sirju at the singhasan (podium) performing a yajna

Chapter 7

Sirju's Commitment to the Larger Community

We make a living by what we get, but we make a life by what we give.

— Winston Churchill

Race

In the course of its political history, Guyana had been dogged by tensions between the two races which together made up over ninety percent of the population – peoples of Indian and African ancestry. While the source for the tense relations between the two groups have been linked back to the days of British colonialism, they were later exacerbated by Guyana's political leaders for the purpose to gain support.

Pt Sirju's relations with the African community transcended racial barriers through his ability to see the good in each person, irrespective of race. He carried on friendly relationships with all members from this community. Some visited for him to pray for their sick or for their infants. He saw them as he would the people of his own race and religion. Clay, a member of this community, worked on a boat, which meant that he was away from home for long periods at a time. During his absence, he left his car at Pt Sirju's home for safe keeping, also authorising him to use at will. This was but one example of the easy relationship Pt Sirju maintained with everyone around. During yajnas, or other religious occasions, Africans were welcome to attend and be a part of the event.

In 1963, tensions between the races erupted into riots affecting most of the country. During this period, Pt Sirju suffered the death of his brother and a physical attack on his mother. However, he did not attribute the problems to a race, but to the prevailing dissensions within the country. He continued to treat his African neighbours with love and friendship.

Corbin, an African gentleman living nearby in the village of Anns Grove, was purported to be a god son of Pt Sirju. While this may not have been entirely true, Corbin and Pt Sirju had a close, friendly relationship. Pt Sirju was available to people from all religious backgrounds.

Prabhudyal Beepatnath (Chili) 70, a Christian from Clonbrook, knew Pt Sirju since birth. He had this to say about him:

> *He was highly respected in the Hindu, Christian, Muslim and Arya Samaj communities; he preached about the universality of god and that all religions are equal and just different paths to god. I always enjoyed his charisma and preaching; he was a tireless social worker who always had the village at heart.*

In 1982, Swami Sadhaka Rajadeva Alahan was visiting Guyana from India. He held a religious discussion at the Hindu College, Cove and John Ashram on the occasion of Shiv Raatri. Pt Sirju attended the event, and, impressed with the Swami's lecture, invited him to his home in Clonbrook. Swami Alahan who was of Caucasian descent, subsequently followed up with a couple of visits to Pandit's home where he held religious discourses that were attended by adults and children in the community.

Sirju's Commitment to the Larger Community

In inviting the Swami to his village to address the people, Pt Sirju was continuing on his quest to not only be enlightened, but to offer the same opportunity to those around him. As he looked at the Swami, he did not see a race, a Caucasian; what he was seeing was someone who possessed a unique gift that would be a blessing to receive and share.

Community Responsibilities

Pt Sirju's responsibilities were to the larger as well as the spiritual community. He also believed in the strength of solidarity, and that great results could be obtained when communities united for a worthy cause. Whether the community's needs were spiritual, financial or structural, Pt Sirju always did what he could to help.

More than fifty percent of Guyanese live along the Atlantic coast on land that lies six feet below sea level. In the nineteen seventies high tides inundated the villages of Bee Hive and Clonbrook. The concrete walls that were built to keep the tides at bay proved to be inadequate. One of the residents, Mrs Kaiser, gathered some of the women together to visit nearby villages to raise funds for a prayer service.

With the funds that they collected, the residents made elaborate preparations including a huge tent that they setup at the Clonbrook beach. Food items and offerings of mohan bhog (g) were prepared and carried to the beach. Seven women, one from each village took part in the worship of Ganga Ma (g). Pt Sirju officiated at the worship. Shortly after, a tall wall of sand accumulated along the beach, lining the walls and keeping the water from flowing over. Everyone was left wondering where the sand had come from, and amazed at the miracle!

Chantamonie Minkoo related how he invited Pandit on a yearly basis to perform a Surujnarayan (g) Puja for him. On this particular Sunday morning, it was arranged for Pt Sirju to arrive early at his home so that the puja would be finished by sunrise. Pt Sirju arrived at 5:30 a.m. while it was still dark. The gate was locked and the house was lit. However, Chantamonie's family was in the home busy cooking, in preparation for the puja and did not hear Pandit calling out, or him rattling the gate. So Pt Sirju decided to return home and go back to Chantamonie's home at daybreak.

He was in better luck the second time as the gate was open. Chantamonie told him that he thought he would have come earlier. He remembers Pandit's hearty laughter as he related how he came earlier and the gate was locked. On his way home, the neighbourhood dogs tried to attack him. He ran for a while on his way home and was fortunate the dogs stopped following him. Chantamonie appreciated the great lengths Pandit went to serve his community and help with the preparations so that he would fulfill his yajman's desire of having the puja finished by sunrise. His love for the people and God was great and he was willing to risk his own well being in order to be of service.

Advise Couple on Psychic Visit

A couple from the village discovered that some of their gold jewellery was missing. Their suspicions immediately rested on a family member, but they wanted to confirm their theory by consulting a psychic.

The psychic, after listening to their account, assured them that she could help. Consulting with her tea leaves, she confirmed that she could see a vivid image of the person who the couple had suspected. The couple wanted a second opinion. They invited Pt Sirju to accompany them on a second visit to the psychic. They trusted his insight, and wanted to hear his opinion of the psychic's revelations. Pt Sirju attempted to dissuade the couple, but they were convinced that the psychic could help them clarify their doubts. During their first visit, the couple had described their suspect to the psychic. Pt

Sirju, sensing potential danger to someone who could be wrongly accused, had decided to accompany the couple to help dismiss or validate assumptions of guilt.

Arriving at the psychic's, she observed that she could immediately sense that they were in trouble. Pt Sirju, nimble on his feet as usual, started to relate to the psychic that he was facing a serious problem at home; his wife had deserted him, and he was left to look after many children. He was anxious to know whether his wife would return home. The psychic asked him to look into the jar of tea leaves she was holding, then said to him: *there she is, can you see her? She would never return home.*

On the return trip home, the discussion centered around the fictitious story he had made up to prove his point to them: that it was possible for the psychic to be misleading as well as misled. While this lone episode is not an indictment of psychics, it shows the lengths Pt Sirju went to defend individuals who may not have been in a position to defend themselves. He had a knack for concocting the type of shrewd circumstances when simple logic failed to bring home a point.

Altruism

In 1987, he visited Guyana to attend a yajna sponsored by his godson Ragnauth Singh. The organising committee for the yajna had selected Pt Sirju to be the head Pandava, a role of honour. This role provided close support and guidance to the officiating priest and other pandavas and srotas at the yajna.

Pt Sirju observed that a local priest, Pt Latchminarine Sharma, had arrived early to prepare for the auspicious event. Pt Sharma had engaged himself in the preparatory rituals to purify the atmosphere, venue and participants in accordance with injunctions from the Hindu scriptures. This included the jhandi ceremony he performed the day before the yajna. Pt Sirju, impressed with Pt Sharma's dedication to the event, advised the organisers to choose Pt Sharma as their head pandava, as he was the better choice for the role. He encouraged everyone to excel, always placing their interests above his own. Therefore, he had a great impact on many.

Harold Kowlessar from Clonbrook describes Pt Sirju's tribute to those he touched during the routine conduct of his life as:

> *I have developed a love for Satsang (g) mainly because of being influenced by Pandit Ji. He gifted to me a copy of the Bhagavad Gita on the very day I immigrated which I greatly treasure. In all our association, everything Pt Sirju passed on was a 'teaching moment', lovingly expressed, like from a father to a son. I recently found a copy of a letter which was sent to me, dated April 26, 1993 in which my brother Saisnarine (Sais) wrote a special letter of recommendation to then Minister Of Education, Sport & Culture, Dr Dale Bisnauth. At the time, Sais was a Lecturer at UG (University of Guyana). I quote:*

> "Through the medium of your office, I am recommending the following persons who, by dint of selfless and dedicated service to the people of Guyana, may be considered for appropriate National Awards to be announced in the Independence anniversary celebrations. In doing so, I am expressing the sentiments of thousands of Guyanese who feel strongly that these persons should have been honored long ago. Pandit Sirju Persaud (presently residing in Canada). A distinguished Hindu Priest for over 40 years who has given dedicated service to the people of Guyana. Also, a dynamic voluntary social worker."

Financial Altruism

Pt Sirju seemed to convey an impression of wealth. He received constant requests for financial help, which led Dalia to suggest that

Sirju's Commitment to the Larger Community

he was likely sending a message of being well off which was far from accurate. His response was that they were in a position to help as they likely had more than the person asking for assistance.

The impression that he conveyed either came from his general deportment or from a reputation of never turning someone away. Those asking for help would have been surprised to learn that Pt Sirju was by no means wealthy, but that his family also needed to budget wisely to make ends meet. The generosity extended beyond a readiness to provide financial aid. He deferred to the other person whenever he saw that there was an opportunity for that person to benefit.

And when he was offered financial help, he never forgot the favor. Pt Sirju lived with Dalia and their ten children in a small three bedroom home for many years. In spite of the small size, many guests stayed at the home, some for the duration of many weeks. In the early seventies, Pt Sirju embarked on a project to build a larger home for his family. Before the home could be completed however, his funds ran out.

Forced to seek means of obtaining cash to complete painting of the home, he approached a relative with a request to borrow $5000.00. This was considered a large amount in those days. The lender however, had total confidence that Pt Sirju would repay, and saw no need to prepare documents to confirm the transaction.

Pt Sirju never forgot the kindness of the relative. He would often recount the incident praising the kindness of the lender; as he would repeat similar circumstances where someone did him a good turn. He remained indebted for the rest of his life if any one ever offered to help him.

As everyone who knew him remarked, humility was his trademark personality trait. Forever grateful for any kindness or favors anyone gave him, he would remark, *I can't ever forget*. He told of many stories of help offered him, but seldom mentioned what he did for others. In a similar vein, if someone did not treat him right, he would make excuses for the shoddy person's behaviour.

Insurance

In the course of his travels as a priest throughout Guyana, Pt Sirju came to understand the financial peril that many people faced. Most families relied on the income of one spouse and did not have any financial means if that spouse was ill or died. Guyana's economy was primarily supported through rice and sugar in the early nineteen sixties. If the spouse who worked in this field were to suddenly die, they left their family with no other means to support themselves. RRSPs, retirement funds, and stock portfolios were not available to most of the residents of Guyana at this time, so the widow was often left destitute.

Pt Sirju felt as if life insurance could provide families with many options that included, repayment of debt, replacement in income and planning one's estate. He saw the opportunity to educate the general population on the importance of insurance in their lives, and took up a part time vocation in selling Life Insurance policies.

Dr Budhendranauth Doobay recalled the period when his brother in law Pt Sirju was an insurance broker in Guyana. On his way to meet with the clients, Pt Sirju would pick up Dr Doobay to visit the client to perform their physical examination. Dr Doobay stated that Pt Sirju was always very kind to the clients and was not doing it for the money but always had the client's best interest at heart. He took the opportunity to educate the community about insurance and its importance in their lives.

At the time, there was a deep-seated distrust of everything related to insurance, and it was not easy to convince most people on the value of owning an insurance policy. But Pt Sirju's determination and patience in explaining the benefits of the appropriate coverage helped assuage some of their distrust. There were many instances where his persistence in getting people to sign up eventually succeeded. In one such incident, after listening to Pt Sirju's description of the benefits that insurance will bring to him, the potential client asked him to return another day. The reason he said, was to spend some time to study the information provided in order to make the right decision. The man's thinking was that as Pt Sirju lived a fairly long distance away, he would not want to waste his time to return back to the home. However, to the man's distress, Pt Sirju was back at the appointed day and time. As Pt Sirju arrived at the man's home, the latter requested his children to inform the visitor that their father was not at home. The ploy did nothing to detract Pt Sirju from his objective, and after his persistence, the man eventually ended up taking out an insurance policy, something for which the man and his family were grateful for in later years.

A client at the time – Pt Omanand Persaud, Queens, NY - related his experience:

> *In the late 1950's or early 1960's, I met Pt Sirju for the 1st time. I was the Trust Officer in the Attorney General's Ministry in Guyana, when Panditji approached me in his capacity as an insurance salesman. I had always resisted buying insurance from the many agents with whom I had previously spoken, but the manner in which Panditji spoke, and his knowledge of insurance and the confidence he exuded were enough to convince me as to the necessity to have insurance coverage – something I never regretted. I gave Panditji several leads and he ended up selling insurance to all the persons whom I suggested. They all informed me that they purchased insurance from him because of his modesty, gentleness, simplicity and honesty.*

A diplomat as well, Pt Sirju was well able to negotiate the best plan from the insurance company for the people of his community. Many clients across the country received the added comfort of knowing that their dependents would be taken care of after their passing.

In addressing this need, he developed into a highly successful insurance sales agent, and in the mid nineteen sixties, was awarded top salesman, producing sales in the order of multi millions. The picture shows him receiving his award, which included a Certificate of Achievement and a gold pendant, presented by a representative of his insurance company, Caribbean Atlantic Life. The event took place in the rooftop garden of Chase Manhattan Bank in Georgetown, Guyana.

Top Insurance Salesman Award

As with any other task that he took on, small or large, there was the same degree of attention and effort that he exercised, giving his best, and in the process attaining excellence!

Deaths and funerals

Cowminer— the name by which one villager was known, probably because he was once a cowherd – was in his mid sixties when he moved to the village with his family. He did not know many people in the village, but sensed that Pt Sirju would welcome him unconditionally. Returning from a visit to the doctor's one day,

Sirju's Commitment to the Larger Community

he stopped at Pt Sirju's home, complaining of feeling unwell. He wanted to take a rest before resuming the walk to his home, about half mile away.

Pt Sirju observed that the man was looking too feeble to walk home. He seemed to be too sick to travel even by boat, were his family wanting to take him to their home at the back dam. Pt Sirju consulted with Dalia of his intentions to invite Cowminer into the home. The plan was for him to rest until the afternoon when his wife and son would take him home. Pt Sirju guided Cowminer up into the home, and with the help of Dalia, setup a bed in one corner of the living room, so that he could lie down and be comfortable.

After about an hour, Pt Sirju checked on the man and saw that he seemed to be lying too still for comfort. He called on a neighbour Louis Veira, who was older and experienced in situations such as this, to check the man for a pulse. The neighbour, on checking the man's pulse, discovered that there was none – he had passed on. Pt Sirju and Dalia were in disbelief that the man had died so suddenly. The man's family was sent for, his wife and four children rushed in, neighbours rushed in, the house was now packed with the sympathisers and the curious.

Cowminer was not a relative to Pt Sirju, but he was a member of the ramayana group that sang at the temple, and therefore a member of Pt Sirju's congregation. Pt Sirju considered the family's dire circumstances and small remote home, and volunteered to have the two nights' wake and funeral conducted from his home. Pt Sirju was a priest of thirty three when this event occurred. For him, a deep sense of compassion was already a way of life.

Another villager named *Mother* – the name by which she was known to all in the village – was a close friend of Chameli's. Their parents had travelled together from India in the same boat. Mother lived alone, as her parents were long gone. She was a regular visitor to Pt Sirju's home, where she was treated as a family member. One day, the neighbours noticed that there were no signs of her that day. They went in to her home to check on her and found her lifeless body.

Because of their close relationship, Pt Sirju assumed the role of a son in completing arrangements for the wake and funeral. He arranged the shraddha ceremony to be performed at his home according to her wishes. Shraddha is a prayer service performed thirteen days after passing of the deceased, for peace of the soul. The priest who was called in to officiate at the rites, offered that the old lady must have done something worthwhile in her life – to have such a good man as Pt Sirju conduct her rites.

Opening His Home to Others

Because of his care for others, Pt Sirju's modest three bedroom home in Clonbrook was a busy household. The home contained one large and two small bedrooms which accommodated him and his wife and ten children. Friends of Pt Sirju from the city of Georgetown asked if their daughter could stay in his house while she attended school nearby. Most, if not all people, would have said, *sorry, it's too crowded and we're filled to capacity,* but not him. Not only did the girl come to live in the home, she was given a bedroom of her own, leaving the rest of the family to sleep crammed in the two other rooms and living room. He just couldn't say no to someone asking a favor.

Pt Sirju's daughter Basso related that as an adult, every conversation she had with her father elicited from him a new prayer or a new story, usually with some humour attached. Irrespective of the reason for the conversation in the first place, conversations with him always veered to some aspect of spirituality. One prayer that he repeated often was:

> Maatri devo bhava, Pitri devo bhava
> Aacharya devo bhava, Atithi devo bhava

Sirju's Commitment to the Larger Community

> Treat your Mother, Father and
> Teacher as equal to God.
> So also, treat your guest as God.

As this was Pt Sirju's belief, no visitor to his home would be allowed to leave without first enjoying some refreshments.

At the more extreme end of the spectrum on generosity, he would accommodate in his home complete strangers who begged lodging for a night or two. A story he laughingly related many years later describes the stay of one such visitor.

The man whom he had never met before visited Pt Sirju's home, begging to stay the night as he didn't have any accommodations. Pt Sirju could not say no to the man. (His wife Dalia, on the other hand, was more concerned, as neither of them knew this person, and the home was already crowded with small children). Later that night as they were getting ready to go to sleep, Pt Sirju said that something about the man gave him an uneasy feeling. A quick thinker, he started a conversation with the stranger, telling him that his face looked familiar, and that he believed he had seen him before. At which, as Pt Sirju retold, the man's expression immediately changed. It took on a questioning uncertain look. To the man's intense consternation, Pt Sirju said to him, *I know where I saw you man, it was in jail!*

On hearing this, the man was somewhat relieved in that here he had met a fellow jail-bird. Pt Sirju's misgivings were confirmed when the man responded that, *Pandit you been in jail too? What you went for?* Of course Pt Sirju had never been to jail, but in order to find out more about his visitor, he responded that yes, he had once been to prison. Whatever the reason, Pt Sirju concocted to relate to him, the man countered that his offence was breaking and entering! That was the end of any sleep for Pt Sirju, as he kept vigil all night praying for morning to arrive early. Of course this incident did not deter him from continuing to assist anyone who came to the home seeking help.

Pt Sirju was able to put his fear to the side in order to help others. Chantamonie Minkoo recollected Pt Sirju's fearlessness even during the 1963 racial disturbances in Guyana. At that time, there were many violent attacks and murders and the entire country was in a state of tension. Properties were also being destroyed. On many occasions, Indians and Africans left their homes to temporarily move in with their friends from the other race group to prevent the arsonists from targeting their homes.

In some cases, Africans and Indians left their homes to resettle in other villages where the numbers of their group dominated. There was a curfew in place in affected communities but that did not help much in preventing the violence. Chantamonie related that everyone was too scared to leave their homes but Pt Sirju continued to go out and perform pujas for people either by walking, cycling or taking a taxi. He observed that *Pandit Sirju risked his life to serve, and dedicated himself at all costs.*

A Helping Hand

On a quiet Sunday afternoon in the early nineteen sixties, members of the temple youth group were getting ready to perform the Krishna Leela drama in the village of Enmore. Word quickly spread that the home of the drummer, Mujhay Hoolas, had caught on fire. The home was grazed to the ground despite all efforts to douse the fire. Later, the cause of the fire was traced to a faulty electrical connection.

Pt Sirju quickly galvanised the community members to assist in his efforts to rebuild the home. He started a fundraising drive. Accompanied by community members, he travelled to the many villages to solicit funds. His son Ravi recalls going with him all the way to Mahaicony, a village about ten miles away to ask for help.

Back in Clonbrook, he met with Fayuz Baksh, who owned and operated a home construction company, to discuss the project of rebuilding the home. Baksh kindly volunteered in the rebuilding of Hoolas' home, all done for no pay! Pt Sirju was the driving force in spearheading efforts to get the homeless family back on their feet quickly. This was his typical response when anyone in the community was in distress or in need; he was ready to take the lead to provide the required assistance.

Undeterred

One night around 9.00 pm, Pt Sirju was returning from a puja he had performed in neighbouring Unity. The taxi dropped him off at the public road, it was pitch dark and he started his walk through the village of Bee Hive, on his way to perform a maticore (g) ceremony. Out of the darkness, two guys brandishing a machete jumped out blocking his path.

When they warned that they were going to kill him, he wanted to know the reason, as he told them that he was unaware of any wrong that he could have committed. They then realized that it was Pt Sirju, as it was very dark they had not recognized him earlier. They apologized and let him go after telling him that he was a good man and that they would not hurt him.

Naturally, Pt Sirju was shocked and raced through the mud as it had rained heavily. His slippers got stuck in the mud but he did not bother to remove them. He continued his journey barefoot. When he reached the home of the family, it was already late and they wanted to know what took him so long. He narrated the incident he had just encountered ending that he was lucky to be alive. The sight of his muddy feet and his clothing splashed with mud explained it all.

That incident did not deter him from walking and cycling late in the night for many years after. He felt an obligation to serve and be with the people.

Living with Purpose

We must be the change we wish to see in the world.
— Mahatma Gandhi

The Guru's Guru

Despite his own growing reputation, Pt Sirju never forgot his own guru. Pt Ramphair, together with his wife, would often times spend a period of days at Pt Sirju's home, either to officiate over a religious function, or sometimes just to spend time with his godson. Pt Sirju loved these visits and looked forward to them with eagerness, as if expecting a long lost friend. He was steadfast in worship of his Guru, who was also his mentor and a friend.

Pt Sirju's children developed the same love and respect for their father's mentor. They enjoyed his visits, as he was a spry and intelligent individual with a jovial personality. They all spent many hours in conversation and laughter with him.

Pt Ramphair was a diabetic, the disease eventually led to him developing gangrene in one of his legs. It became necessary to amputate the leg. During his confinement at the Georgetown Public hospital, Pt Sirju was insistent that all of his children visit with Pt Ramphair at the hospital. Son Jaiwant, who was squeamish at any faint signs of blood, reluctantly agreed to the visit. As Jaiwant had feared, while standing beside Pt Ramphair's bed and talking to him, he fell in a faint.

Following the amputation, Pt Sirju was relentless in pursuing all options to get his godfather back on his feet. In discussing these options with the attending doctors, he was advised that, fitted with a prosthetic leg, the patient would soon be able to walk. Pt Sirju set about to find out the process to obtain the prosthesis, and eventually he was able to organize the means to obtain one. Through his unfailing efforts, his Guru was able to get back on his feet after being fitted with a prosthetic leg. The episode illustrated the extent of the devotion Pt Sirju held for his Guru.

Sirju's Commitment to the Larger Community

Swami - Bharat Sevashram Sangha Canada

Pt Sirju was unwavering in the protection of his religion and its followers. The following story provided by Swami Bhajananda of the Bharat Sevashram Sangha Canada, illustrates Pt Sirju's dedication to a cause:

> *Om Naa-raa-ya-naaya Vidmahey*
> *Vasudevaaya Dheemahi*
> *Tannoh Vishnu Pracho-dayaat.*
>
> *We contemplate on the supreme abode of all.*
> *We meditate upon the effulgent yet unmanifest Being.*
> *May that all-pervading Lord ever*
> *inspire us to His lotus feet.*

Initially, through his children who were students of the Hindu College in Cove & John, on the East Coast of Demerara, Pandit Ji came into recognition in the eyes of Rector/Founder of the Hindu College and the Cove & John Ashram - the late Param Pujya Srimat Swami Purnanandaji Maharaj. As a parent, Pt Sirju could always be relied on by Swamiji for his support and co-operation. In 1966, the late Swami Brahmanandaji Maharaj came to know Pandit Sirju and his family and took a special likeness and admiration for PanditJi and his family and his religious work in the village in Clonbrook.

In the year 1966, as a Brahmachari, I would be sent by Guruji-Swami Purnanandaji Maharaj to the home of Pandit Sirju very often to consult with him on various religious matters affecting the Hindus and of General Public interest. When Guruji-Swami Purnanandaji Maharaj wanted to include discussions on the Ramayana on Shiva Ratri as a form of education to the Hindu masses, he invited Pandit Sirju to the Ashram and sought his opinion. Panditji, without hesitation, supported the inclusion of

Ramayana Sammelan advising Guruji of its value in the enlightenment of the general Public.

In the early nineteen seventies, when the then Government nationalised all Private secondary schools and wanted to use the school buildings of the Ashram for various community activities, the Ashram premises and buildings were listed to be taken by the Government for such use. Swami Purnananda sent me with a request for Panditji to visit him on an urgent matter. After Guruji had outlined the distressing situation, Pandit Sirju suggested to Guruji - Swami Purnanandaji to start performing Hanuman Jhandi in the buildings as a means to religiously occupy them. Panditji started the pujas and dutifully came to the Ashram for many, many years to perform Hanuman Jhandi, thus preventing the Government from taking the Ashram buildings for Village Council activities.

Pandit Sirju Persaud Misir was a philanthropist, dedicated Hindu Priest and Leader, especially in the Village of Clonbrook and in Toronto, and a Guru to many to whom he has taught the Puja Bidhi (performing Hindu rites and rituals). He was always ready to sacrifice personal comfort for the sake of others, for in his very life he reflected the teachings of the Holy Ramayana and Bhagavad Gita.

In conclusion as I write these sketches on the life of Pandit Sirju Persaud Misir, it comes to mind that his life and works fit in with this verse of the Gita Mahatmya:

Geetaartham dhyaayate nityam
Kritvaa Karmaani Bhuurisah
Jivanmukta sa vi-gyey-yo Dehaante Paramam Padam.

He is to be regarded a Jivanmukta,
who constantly meditates on the meaning of the Gita
in the midst of performing his Karma without respite.
He attains the supreme state at the fall of the body.

Sirju's Commitment to the Larger Community

> *Pandit Sirju Persaud loved the Bhagavad Gita and I personally had the grand privilege to hear him read one of the best Gita Yajnas in Clonbrook on the East Coast of Demerara by the Railway line in the nineteen seventies. The yajna was sponsored by Thakur Persaud, his brother Sewdat from Toronto and their parents.*
>
> *May Bhagwan Krishna keep his soul in Eternal bliss for the Lord made him His instrument of His peace. Where there was hatred, he sowed love and where there was injury, pardon.*
>
> *Om Shanti. Shanti. Shanti (Peace).*

Open to All Religions

Pt Sirju's belief was the Hindu belief that all religions lead to the same God. As Mahatma Gandhi, one of the most well known of Hindus said, if one is a Christian, be a good Christian; if a Hindu, be a good Hindu; if a Muslim, be a good Muslim. Pt Sirju's objective was to instil this belief in the members of his community; the understanding that their religion preached an omnipotent, omniscient, omnipresent and loving God, who loved and provided for all.

In the early sixties, a Christian Brother had started to conduct religious services on the ground floor of his home. The Christian Brother's service was scheduled to start at 8pm with singing of the hymn, *Follow Jesus, no turning back...* Villagers living around the neighborhood had complained about the use of high volume loudspeakers that the Brother used to conduct the service. They believed that it reflected a lack of respect for all those who lived in the area. On listening to the complaints, the Hindu Youth organisation (HYO) members convened a meeting to discuss the methods that the Christian Brother had adopted. To try and curb the Christian Brother's methods, they planned to meet at a destination neighbouring the Christian Brother's home in time for his 8pm service time, and to then begin chants of, *Follow Rama, no turning back*....

Pt Sirju apprised of the situation, arrived at the scene appalled. He condemned the actions of the youths, maintaining that the behaviour was misguided.

Through Pt Sirju's direction, a team was formed consisting of two senior members of the HYO. The team was instructed that instead of retaliating against the Christian Brother's services by disrupting them with Hindu chants, they should instead resolve differences through civil means. This meant first of all, they should follow-up with the Christian Brother about the noise level from his services that the neighborhood was complaining about. And secondly, if there was a concern that the purpose of the services was to convert Hindus to Christianity, then the team could help to clarify any specific issues or questions a potential convertee harbored regarding their Hindu faith. In this manner of providing instruction on the teachings of their religion, they could persuade the people to remain true to their Hindu birth; and explain why they didn't need to convert to another religion in order to pray to God.

The occurrence with the hindu youths, intrusive but peaceful likely gave cause for self-reflection from the Christian brother. Right after the incident, he turned down the volume on the speakers. His services continued in a quiet, peaceable manner. The mood in the village regained its normal courteous calm where the Hindus, Muslims and Christians lived without any conflicts.

The temple youths shared the tolerance that Hindus have for all religions, but they believed that one did not have to convert from their religion to realise God. Their leader, Pt Sirju, too never objected to someone converting to another religion. But he always wanted to make sure they were educated and provided with all the relevant information before taking that step. And, if someone belonged to another religion, neither he nor the temple members saw a need to convert that person to Hinduism.

Ravendra Kowlessar remarked how Pt Sirju had such a rapport with everyone including those of different races and faiths. He was amazed at how up to date Pt Sirju was in all current affairs and how accepting and tolerant he was of others.

Pt Sirju often referred to the words of Swami Vivekananda:

> *All who have actually attained any real religious experience never wrangle over the form in which the different religions are expressed. They know that the soul of all religions is the same and so they have no quarrel with anybody just because he or she does not speak in the same tongue.*

Closest to the Truth

Chandranarain Doobay (Cecil Ram), was a godson of Pt Sirju. Like all Hindus, he believed in reincarnation. In his next birth, he said, he would like to have the same positive personal qualities as Pt Sirju; including the quality of empathy with another.

He recalled an incident when Pt Sirju was the officiating priest at a function he attended. During the ceremony, Pt Sirju called on a speaker who then addressed the audience. At one point during the man's speech, Pt Sirju received a nudge from another member of the audience sitting beside him. The speaker had supposedly just delivered an inaccurate statement, and the purpose of the nudge was to urge the priest to correct the statement. Pt Sirju, as was his style, chose not to interrupt the speaker.

Cecil Ram stressed that Pt Sirju would never criticize or humiliate anyone. He could never hurt anyone. If he wanted to discuss, he would do so in a diplomatic and very quiet manner with only that person, and with no one else around to listen in to the conversation.

Narendra Datt, Pt Sirju's nephew, summed up the reasoning behind this behaviour characteristic of his uncle:

> *He was a very sensitive person who lived his life according to the tenets of the Bhagavad Gita. He taught the principle to refrain from hurting anyone by thought, word or deed. In his practice of truth, he taught that if the primary purpose of the truth is to hurt the feelings of someone, then that truth should not be spoken. However, if the purpose of the truth is to correct an injustice, then that truth should be proclaimed at all levels ...*

Pt Sirju lived according to these extreme tenets.

Roger Rajkumar grew up in the village of Enmore, about ten miles from Clonbrook. Roger lives in Toronto where he owns a computer software consulting firm. His memories of Pt Sirju date back to his childhood days when the latter performed religious functions for the people at Enmore. Roger remembers that one of his relatives Chunku, was particularly selective on who he invited to perform religious functions that he hosted. Chunku was a perfectionist when it came to choosing a priest to conduct his services, he wanted someone who he had the highest regard for. Pt Sirju was his priest of choice, as Chunku admired his dedication to the religion, his simplicity, and integrity. Roger said that he, his nine brothers and three sisters and their families attended many services, yajnas or other pujas in the country that Pt Sirju conducted, as they considered it a treat to listen to his lectures. Roger observed that Pt Sirju was a humble person, who took pride in his priestly work. And in spite of age, he carried on in his duties with excellence.

Roger described Pt Sirju as one who tried to live *closest to the truth,* and that his way of life should be an example worth emulating.

> *Don't wait for the last judgment - it takes place every day.*
> *– Albert Camus*

Shiwala (Altar) at Clonbrook Home

Chapter 8

Fatherhood, Family, and Grandchildren

Your children will see what you are all about by what you live rather than what you say.

– Wayne Dyer

Father

Pt Sirju was a dedicated father and family man. He led his children with a gentle but firm hand. Inasmuch as he counselled and encouraged other parents to make certain their children received a formal education, Pt Sirju spared no pains to ensure his own children's completion of their formal schooling.

Pt Sirju loved music. With his children, as well as the broader community, he was equally influential in the acute interest and virtuosity a few of them acquired in the field of music. Sons Shiv and Anant developed talents as vocalists, Shiv also becoming fluent in playing the harmonium; daughters Kaywala and Chandra established themselves as vocalists, while son Hemant became proficient in playing the drums and tabla (g).

In addition to these 'gifts' that Pt Sirju endowed his children, and the passing on of his core values of compassion and simplicity, Pt Sirju influenced his children by example. In the following section, each of Pt Sirju's ten children highlight their individual relationships with their father.

Raj, Parbatee, Shiv, Kaywala (Kay), Hemant and Ravi live in Toronto. Basso travels back and forth between Toronto and Trinidad, her four sons now residing in Toronto, while her husband still practises medicine in Trinidad. Pt Sirju's two other sons – Anant and Pt Jaiwant live with their families in Queens and Long Island respectively. Chandra – Pt Sirju's daughter - is the only child still living with her family in Guyana.

Raj – Equal Opportunity Dad

A lack of the opportunities to complete his formal education no doubt influenced Pt Sirju's determination that his children should not suffer the same fate. To align wishes with resolve, he was determined to provide his children with the necessary resources to pursue their academic goals.

In 1971, when his eldest child, Raj, left Guyana to attend Mc Master University in Hamilton, Canada, Pt Sirju bucked the trend of an Indian father from a rural community. In allowing and encouraging a daughter to travel alone to a foreign country in order to obtain a good education, Pt Sirju showed that he was an equal opportunity father.

Pt Sirju kept in regular communication with Raj, by travelling the twenty miles to make pay phone calls from the Guyana Telecommunications Corporation (GTC) building in the city of Georgetown. He would arrive there as early as 4 a.m., having left home in the early hours to join the line at GTC. If, as often happened, he couldn't get through on that day because of usual quirks in the telephone system, he would repeat the process again the next day until he got through to her.

Raj arrived in Canada as a foreign student. This meant that costs for tuition were a multiple of what a Canadian resident paid. In addition, the Guyana currency was valued at a third the Canadian dollar at the time. These factors were no deterrent to Pt Sirju. At one time, he needed to make a short term loan from a friend in the village in order to fund his daughter's expenses, but Pt Sirju was determined to find the means to pay for his daughter's education.

Parbatee – Encouraged Children in Their Efforts in Academic Achievements

In 1974, his daughter Parbatee wrote the GCE Ordinary Level, an examination administered externally by the University of London, England. As word came that the results were posted, Pt Sirju readily left for the Ministry of Education in the city of Georgetown to collect her report.

Parbatee remembers the pleasure in Pt Sirju's expression vividly. Like any dad, he was pleased when any of his children excelled academically. The next day he accompanied her to the Bygeval Multilateral High School in Mahaica, about five miles from their home, to apply for a teaching job. The headmaster at the school immediately accepted her application, telling them that she needed to register with the Ministry of Education in the city of Georgetown. Pt Sirju eagerly drove Parbatee to Georgetown and back to the High School all on the same day. Parbatee wanted to start her teaching assignment without further wait, and Pt Sirju, truly dedicated to the causes of his children, was there to help.

Parbatee also recalled the early morning commutes accompanying her father to the cable and wireless building in Georgetown to connect with her sister Raj in Canada. Her father had discovered that it was easier to get a telephone connection in the early morning hours when the line-up was shorter and reception was clear. Her dad would leave home early in the morning, usually around 4:00 a.m. when it was still very dark and she accompanied him on many occasions. She recalled discussing with her dad how magical it all seemed to her as a young kid to hear someone's voice many thousands of miles away. These are some of the priceless moments she shared with her father.

Parbatee, like her sister Raj, arrived on a student visa to attend university in Canada in 1982. Once again, it was a difficult decision to send off another member of their close-knit family, but her parents were willing to provide the resources so that their children could pursue their dreams for a better education. The parents also trusted their children. They had faith that they had given their children the tools needed to guide them through life's challenges and to be independent in a foreign land.

Parbatee stated that now that her dad is gone and he is not here physically, the decisions and actions that his children take on a daily basis are based on what he would have done in similar situations. The children still think about what he would have liked and what he would have done before making major decisions.

Jaiwant - Pandit

Pt Sirju encouraged students from the village into various professions – doctors, lawyers, accountants, educators, scientists. His children were no less the recipients to similar counsel. Their father fully engaged in assisting them in their choices of a suitable profession. With his father's guidance, son Jaiwant followed in his father's footsteps by taking up the priesthood.

In the year 1990, Pt Jaiwant and his father Pt Sirju officiated together at a Hindu yajna in Minnesota, USA. Pt Sirju officiated on the Friday and Saturday evenings, while Pt Jaiwant presided at the conclusion of the yajna on Sunday morning. The three day yajna, believed to be one of the first events of the kind performed in this state, was sponsored by Pt Sirju's godchildren Ramraj and Rukhmin Singh at their home in Apple Valley Minnesota. The family hosted the sessions as an expression of thanks to God for the blessings that they had received through the years.

Ramraj was celebrating his fiftieth birthday, and his son David, his twelfth. The significance to Ramraj of celebrating his golden anniversary was intensified by the impending initiation of his son in the janeo samskaar (g), followed by the diksha snaan, or christening. At twelve years old, David had approached the age at which Hindu boys are ready to appreciate the significance of the initiation. If, usually with assistance from their parents, the boy has chosen a guru at this age, the christening is done at the same time as the janeo sanskaar. Otherwise, the christening is performed in a separate ceremony later when the individual is ready by choosing a spiritual guide.

David's father Ramraj was initiated in the janeo sanskaar when he was eleven years old, followed by a christening to Pt Sirju during the same ceremony as the initiation. Now, it was David's turn to be initiated. With his parents' guidance, he chose Pt Jaiwant as his guru.

For Pt Jaiwant, the yajna signalled a glorious moment in his career as a Hindu Priest. It was a rare and rewarding honour being given the chance to share the hallowed podium with his charismatic father. The opportunity allowed him to witness at close hand some of the great qualities of his father: his understanding of the depths of Hinduism, his eloquence in translating, his humility and his serene disposition.

Through the guidance of Pt Sirju, his son Pt Jaiwant became a Hindu priest, who, like his father, sought to grow through continuous learning. Pt Jaiwant stumbled on occasions while going through the laborious and intriguing training to become a Hindu priest. He related that as a teacher, Pt Sirju was always very tolerant and full of patience. He never tired of going over the material—over and over again—for the benefit of his student. Pt Sirju stressed the need for proper pronunciation, and eloquent and smooth delivery.

Pt Jaiwant said that he kept in daily contact with his father in Toronto. The topic of conversation inevitably related to aspects of spirituality. He said that Pt Sirju was a man of great humility. In the face of hardships or difficulties, he never complained; but sought divine guidance and support, and therefore, emerged stronger and more peaceful from the experience.

Pt Jaiwant recounted that whenever he visited his father's home in Canada, he saw him often sitting in deep contemplation to God for hours on end, oblivious to all the activity that was going on around him. Pt Sirju had found bliss in the inner self. Pt Jaiwant believed that his father had discovered the art of withdrawal from external sources of desires and wants, which he accomplished through meditation.

He described his father's life as one based on spiritual bliss that is enjoyed only by those capable of self control. Though surrounded by pleasurable and painful objects to disturb the presence of mind, he remained as immovable as a rock, receiving all sensory stimuli with equanimity. His father had acquired peace of mind by slaying its enemies of greed, lust, jealousy, envy, anger, pride and egoism. He did this through dispassion, discrimination and non attachment. These were the teachings of the Bhagavad Gita, a text which Pt Sirju loved, and one that he used as a guide to conduct his life.

Shiv- Career Choices

Pt Sirju's influences and acute interest in music, as well as his community spirit, were traits inherited by his son Shiv. Although his musical interest was sparked by Pt Sirju, Shiv's ability to play the harmonium was mainly self taught, with a few classes that he took much later providing a measure of formal training. While in his twenties, Shiv started a musical band in the Toronto region. He created the band with a purpose of raising funds for charitable organisations in the area.

The band included Shiv, his two siblings Hemant and Kay, and members of the community – Erroll and his sister Savitri Persaud, Teerath and Brahm among a few other artistes. Shiv was a vocalist accompanying himself on the harmonium; Hemant played the drums and tabla; Kay, Savitri, Teerath and Brahm were vocalists; with other artistes on various musical instruments including the guitar; and Erroll as MC.

The band's first event was a concert performance to raise funds for the Toronto branch of the Bharat Sevashram Sangha. This is a worldwide charitable organisation founded in early nineteen hundreds in Kolkata, India by Swami Pranavanandaji Maharaj. In nineteen fifty five, a mission sent by the founder to various countries to revive the tenets of the Vedic (g) culture, arrived in British Guiana. A core philosophy of the mission stressed the concept of service to humanity through devotion, knowledge, meditation and selfless service. The Hindu College, an institution offering secondary school education, as well as education on the Vedic principles, was founded soon after the mission's arrival in the country. Many of Pt Sirju's children attended the school in Guyana. Shiv decided that it was a most appropriate beneficiary for proceeds from the band's first charity effort.

The band performed at many charitable organisations through the years. After its dissolution, Shiv continued to perform at charitable events at the mandir and at other cultural events; often accompanied by Kay and Hemant. Accompanying himself at the harmonium, Shiv performs bhajans and ghazals (g) at community wakes, weddings, pujas and at the Mandirs.

Pt Sirju contemplated the career track of training to become a Hindu priest as a possible option for Shiv. He made this wish known to Shiv while leaving Ottawa on a visit to Guyana. Wanting to have someone available to perform pujas in the community while he was on vacation, he talked with Shiv about the prospect of him taking up the priesthood. He encouraged him by describing the spiritual good the priesthood could bring and wrote out numerous prayers and mantras for Shiv to learn from. Shiv presided at the Sunday service in Ottawa a few times and did a puja once for a resident. However, he showed little interest in pursuing the priesthood. Pt Sirju talked with Shiv again when the family moved to Toronto. He continued to pass along many prayers, but Shiv decided that he was not comfortable or ready for the priesthood.

Shiv graduated with a biochemical engineering diploma in Ottawa but a job in his field was difficult to come by. Pt Sirju and the family had moved from Ottawa to Toronto in the late nineteen eighties, one of the main reasons being the lack of job opportunities for his children in Ottawa. Soon after the move to Toronto, Shiv found a suitable job in a medical lab. It took only a few hours working at the lab before he realised that he was not interested in pursuing a career in the field. He was ill at ease working with the core medical products such as blood that would encompass a major body of the work done in a medical lab.

Shiv's disillusion in his career choice to date, provided an opportune moment for Pt Sirju to discuss possible career options with his son. Pt Sirju had acquired experience in the real estate field by completing a number of successful transactions in Guyana. He sensed that his son would be good in the real estate business since Shiv possessed a strong, independent temperament, which would be an asset at sales. In guiding Shiv to a possible career in real estate, he described the details in the transactions he had negotiated through the years in Guyana, and the financial potential to this career choice.

Following the discussions, Shiv enrolled for real estate courses. He trusted his dad's advice knowing his dad always had the best interest of his children at heart. Shiv progressed into a successful real estate broker with many exclusive memberships and awards in his profession.

Hemant

As a young boy, Hemant had accompanied Pt Sirju on many occasions to the pujas his dad performed. The exposure provided him with many lessons that he drew on in later life. He learnt how to prepare the puja site, determine where the puja should be held and the purpose for each item that was used in the rituals. Whenever the family had a puja to prepare for, Hemant was usually the one who prepared the setup. Accompanying his dad to the religious events gave him a good insight into the Hindu mythology.

As a boy, Hemant was also the frequent courier to deliver Pt Sirju's summons and subsequent minutes of meetings to the temple committee members. The nature of these childhood experiences introduced Hemant to the spirit of community involvement. Pt Sirju's perseverance in the various endeavours were not lost on Hemant who learnt the value of hard work and dedication by observing his father. He saw that in his father's eyes, there were no roadblocks whenever he was called to serve.

Pt Sirju was engaged in each aspect of his children's' lives. As kids, whenever his children were sitting around, he would test their spelling skills. He always wanted to make sure that they were progressing academically. Hemant recalled one such occasion when he was sitting with a sibling and their father on the veranda in the Guyana home. His dad was testing his ability to spell, and after he failed the test, his dad turned to the sibling imploring her with – *please, help this child.*

During boyhood, Hemant had shown a keen interest in playing the drums. Pt Sirju encouraged him to take lessons and enrolled him for classes at the Cultural Centre in Guyana. Hemant later took tabla lessons in Canada which allowed him to play both the tabla and drums. Hemant plays the two instruments at religious functions in Canada and New York whenever he attends these events.

At the time when Hemant was evaluating his career options, Pt Sirju encouraged him to take up insurance. Hemant had completed an accounting designation, and his dad thought that insurance would complement his accounting background. Pt Sirju provided him with tips and ideas on how to increase referrals. Hemant works as a Financial Advisor where knowledge of insurance is one of his strengths.

Pt Sirju never ceased to influence his children in a positive manner.

Fatherhood, Family, and Grandchildren

Kay and the Band

Pt. Sirju's daughter Kay is a vocalist who performs at pujas, weddings, funerals or other community events. She said that her dad always praised and encouraged her singing whenever he was in the audience.

Kay said that when she was a little girl, and her dad returned from one of his trips to the city, he would have a brown bag with goodies for the family. He knew exactly what each of his family liked. She said that she was the first one to search the bag. Pt Sirju would buy not only for his children but for any visitors.

When Kay attended high school in Guyana at the Mahaica Multilateral, her father organised her travel arrangements with drivers in the village. These were taxi owners who normally took fares to that part of the countryside. He was an attentive father, and it was important that his daughter was not left stranded on the roadside.

She said that later when she got her own family, and Pt Sirju visited, her husband Khemraj cherished the times he sat and had lengthy spiritual conversations with her dad. If they watched some television shows, her dad would remark that they should be more discriminating in the type of shows they watched. He inspired them to make better choices.

Whenever the family got together, her dad looked happy that everyone was having a good time. He enjoyed the grand kids' song and dance performances and would have a good laugh. Kay often senses that her dad is still watching over the family. Looking at his picture at the altar, he appears to fit right in there - just where he belongs.

Anant

When Anant was a small boy, Pt Sirju towed him at the back of his bicycle as he travelled through the various villages of Unity, Hope

Estate, Dochfour and Stratsphey to perform pujas. Anant, Pt Sirju's oldest son, assisted with the fire baba role. On one occasion, when his dad was presiding at a seven day yajna in Stratsphey, a village about ten miles west of Clonbrook, Anant stayed with him for the entire week. At that young age, Anant also partook in salt free meals for the week as he stayed at the same home with his dad and the srotas. Thus through his father, he learnt from a tender age the discipline of observing a strict diet.

As was the case with his siblings, Anant learnt to sing bhajans at an early age. He developed into a good vocalist and performed at religious functions. While attending Teacher's Training College in Guyana, Anant organized a Holi show on behalf of the school, during which he was one of the singing acts. Both his organizing and vocal skills were heavily influenced by Pt Sirju's guide.

Anant remembered how thrilling it was for him to accompany his dad to musical concerts such as when Kishore Kumar, a popular playback singer from India on a world tour, performed in Guyana.

In 1981, Anant emigrated to the Unites States of America to marry his fiancée who lived in Queens, New York. Pt Sirju wanted to drive Anant to the airport, but on the same day he was scheduled to perform a puja for a family in Champagne, Mahaicony. Faced with the conflicting timing of the two events, he arranged with the family in Mahaicony and another priest, Pt Ganesh to substitute for him. A loving father, Pt Sirju never missed an important event in his children's lives in spite of busy involvement in community activities.

Chandra

Chandra, a trained school teacher, was the only child of Pt Sirju's who remained in Guyana. She retired from teaching at a young age to carry on a hardware business with her husband. Like most of her siblings, she acquired the art as a vocalist from an early age through her father's guidance and regular practice, at home and at

Fatherhood, Family, and Grandchildren

the temple. Chandra sings bhajans at pujas, weddings, funerals, and other functions in Guyana.

These are Chandra's words about her father:

> *Growing up in Clonbrook, being the second eldest daughter of Pandit Sirju and Dalia Persaud, was a "life long experience" to say the least. Myself and siblings were very lucky, for we were growing up during difficult times in the then British Guyana, when political disturbances and turmoil were at optimum levels, but that did not deter my Pitagee (g) on his quest to ensure we become staunch devotees of Satya Sanatan Dharma. Although society was unraveling in almost every section within the country, my father maintained his composure and mandir ethics to ensure that those disturbances had miniscule impact to our family values and pursuit of greater heights.*
>
> *I remember one particular occasion during riots in the country when my mother and us children were sent away to my nani's home at Annandale village on the east coast of Guyana, so as to ensure that our safety and security was not compromised. Mandir activities were also a fixture in my life because of my father's insistence that our family passed the baton to keep the flag of sanatan dharma flying high through the generations.*
>
> *There were other aspects of family life where Pitagee played an essential role to ensure that myself, brothers and sisters turned out to be well rounded individuals. One instance was when he was an insurance salesman, we made frequents trips with him to the ancient county of Berbice. There, he would allow us to engage in youth type activities such as shopping and touring historical sites in the town of New Amsterdam, always ensuring that we were well taken care of.*
>
> *Another quality that he possessed that left a lasting impression in me was his willingness to help people in need. I remember one day when he was on vacation in Guyana, he just got home from conducting a funeral service, when*

someone came to "open book" – seeking spiritual guidance on a matter. I had already taken out his lunch but he said, "Chandra, I cannot fill my stomach knowing someone is awaiting that is suffering" he forgot about lunch and proceeded with his spiritual guidance. After he completed his rituals, he related to me that no food can give the type of fufillment that comes from helping others.

Where else can one find such humility and simplicity in a person? With tears flowing from my eyes I can safely say that my father's name will be remembered, wherever the history of Clonbrook and Hinduism is written. It was truly a blessing from birth to have him as a father, for his legacy will live on for generations to come.

Jai Shree Rama - May that Supreme Being grant him everlasting peace.

Basso

Basso described that as a child, she and the entire family would sit together at home to do puja on special occasions. The siblings had a lot of fun, with their dad leading the singing of bhajans and prayers. She also fondly remembers accompanying her father on drives with her siblings. They didn't care whether he was going to meet a prospective insurance client, and that they sometimes needed to wait around in the car for hours while he carried on lengthy conversations with anyone he was fortunate to meet up with. The children knew that if this happened, their dad would always find a way – with treats or a surprise visit - to make up for keeping them waiting. Pt Sirju was well aware of the little things that his children fancied, such as a visit to the ice cream parlour at the Jaipargas's gas station, and he didn't disappoint.

Driving the car, Pt Sirju would start singing bhajans, accompanied by the kids singing along at the top of their voices. The noise attracted attention, but people smiled at the group having fun.

The bhajans were the same ones that Pt Sirju's children continued to sing with their dad as they got older.

After marriage, Basso lived in Trinidad with her husband and four sons. Pt Sirju and Dalia visited them often. Their last holiday in Trinidad was in December 2008. Pt Sirju easily made friends with the plumbers and gardeners who were working at Basso's home. He would start to engage them in conversations at which Dalia needed to caution about him 'gaffing' (g) too much and holding up the job that they were hired to do.

One day during his visit, a couple of contractors were hired to fix some pipes in the home. Pt Sirju pulled up a chair, the contractors stopped their work, and the group began conversing about Pt Sirju's favourite subject – religion. Pt Sirju was oblivious to the fact that the contractors were paid by the hour until Basso was able to help them come to an abrupt conclusion of the discussions. Later in the visit, Pt Sirju learned that Basso's neighbour was sick, so he offered to go and pray for the person although he had never met the man.

Basso said that she called her dad in Toronto anytime she found out that he was at home alone. He never complained about being alone, rather he would say that Lord Krishna was keeping him company. She said that her dad's unstinting faith helped him cross many hurdles in life. He kept this faith to the very end of his days. Basso said that as she watched him being wheeled into the operating theatre for the last time, he was very calm. When the nurse asked if he was scared, he gave his signature laugh and responded, *I leave everything in the hands of the Lord.*

Basso felt blessed to have had Pt Sirju as her father, and she felt that she would be doubly blessed if Pt Sirju is her dad again in some other life time.

Ravi

Ravi, the youngest in the family, had a unique relationship with his father in that he lived with him until Pt Sirju passed away. Pt Sirju was fortunate to see his wish fulfilled for his last son to tie the knot - he died six weeks after Ravi's wedding. At the wedding, Pt Sirju basked in the reunion with the many relatives and friends who attended. Ravi's eulogy at his father's funeral said that Lord Krishna threw many celebrations for his dad prior to his passing and that his (Ravi's) wedding was one of the festivities.

Here are Ravi's words describing his father -

> *I was very fortunate to have a parent as kind, humble and inspiring as my father.*
>
> *As a little boy, I would accompany my father on many of his social duties throughout the villages on the East Coast of Guyana. In some of these encounters he never hesitated to impart his good judgement and encouragement to families and teenagers alike even when he was not asked for such advice. He took a particular interest in the younger children and teenagers because he knew those younger generations are the leaders of tomorrow. His advice was simple but yet profound – follow the advice of your parents, work hard in school to achieve the best results possible and stay on the path of righteousness.*
>
> *Being the youngest of all my siblings, I see the same life-long message being resonated to all of my siblings. My father was particularly keen to know the friends we associated with, our progress in school and the places we frequented for social activities. In so doing, it was not unusual for him to keep pushing all of his children to do the best and be the best to their full God given potential. When grade transcripts were sent out from schools, he always encouraged us to do better. For example, if an A minus was achieved, he typically would encourage us to achieve an A plus the next time around. My father had a keen interest in all of my*

siblings to attend places of worship, in particular religious lectures presented by spiritually inclined individuals. I feel that although he knew that the same lessons were told by these enlightened individuals, he wanted the lessons to be reinforced from another perspective. As I have accompanied him on many such occasions, we would discuss the meanings and relevance of these discourses in the car on our drive back. I still remember the excitement in my father's eyes when I would request a particular book on spirituality or a book on positive development. He would stay up late in the night to find it in his collection or follow up with someone else in his circle of friends to get the book for me. My father believed in 'any means necessary' in being the best person you can be, either by going to lectures, reading spiritual books and/or keeping friends who will uplift and inspire you.

There was never too much for my father to do for anyone in need. There was one occasion when I accompanied him to a religious function in Hope Estate. There we met one individual who needed a taxi from Hope Estate to another village. It was late in the night and so my father on our way back to Clonbrook Village, arranged to have a taxi from Clonbrook to pick up the individual from Hope Estate, even though he only met the individual for a short time. Then there was another occasion when someone wanted to buy a car in order to make a career change but could not find the finances for the purchase. My father without anything to gain from the transaction, quickly used his influence to find a creditor for this individual. These were just a few of the random acts of kindness which defined my father for who he was.

With age he never slowed down from his religious duties. In fact, he was steadfast in his devotion which he exercised every morning before breakfast. He did his prayers with tenacity everyday including on the same day before a fatal slip from his bed. At his tender age of 88 years old he still maintained his connection with the Hindu community

> at large in which he was involved in performing pujas for his closest yajmans. When not performing pujas and morning prayers, my father kept busy by reading religious texts throughout the day from time to time and late into the night. His thoughts were constantly occupied with reflection on the Supreme Being. My father was truly a giant in the field of spirituality and a source of invaluable information for those seeking information on the path of spirituality.

Collective Children's Stories

Collectively, Pt Sirju's children share some of the stories involving their dad, that they either witnessed or were a part of.

Many a violent fight would sporadically erupt among some of the village young men who were inclined to use a more physical style to settle disputes. The causes of these fights were varied. Sometimes, they started from seemingly harmless disagreements that degenerated into violent brawls. At other times, combinations of alcohol and a rash temper escalated into the unexpected, where the combatants resorted to use of weapons such as knives and machetes.

The eruptions were very traumatic for Pt Sirju's children, as they watched their dad fearlessly intervene. He would calmly request the duelling parties to hand over their weapons. While his children would be screaming and terrified for their dad's life, Pt Sirju always succeeded in breaking up the fight. He would follow this up in a conversation with the people involved, if not immediately, at a later time when cooler heads prevailed.

Dealing with Neighbors

A coconut tree growing in Pt Sirju's yard leaned precariously over a neighbor's house. Pt Sirju's older sons overheard their father discussing cutting down the tree, and decided to give him a pleasant surprise. They would first cut the tree down, then share the good news with him after. One son suggested trimming the branches first, but there was disagreement; some in the group believed that this would needlessly prolong the effort. They decided to cut the tree as it was.

Just as the tree was severed, a sudden whiff of wind pushed it onto a neighbor's home. The neighbors, a Portuguese couple, ran out of their home, scared and angry, and started to scream at Pt Sirju's children. The children, realising that they were now in a situation that was beyond their scope to resolve, ran to get help from their father. On learning that his boys had cut the tree, Pt Sirju hastened out to inspect the damage that had been done. As he approached, the neighbours quickly calmed down. They were easily appeased, and assured him that they knew it was an accident. His peaceful demeanour and presence created a calming effect on most people.

Daughter's Engagement

When Pt Sirju's daughter Chandra was getting engaged, the male members of her family, including her father Pt Sirju, travelled to the groom's village for the engagement ceremony. Pt Sirju requested that everyone in the retinue park their vehicles at least three blocks away, so that they could all walk together to the bridegroom's home. He had a flair for tradition, insisting in this case on a solemn procession befitting the occasion. This created a stir, causing all the neighbours to stare out of their windows. The reason for the gawking was explained when one resident yelled across to his neighbor, *.. we never saw so many tall people all at once* - there were about twenty relatives and cousins, many over 6 feet tall.

Kids Ashamed To Let Him Know They Stole From His Land

Pt Sirju owned a plot of land that grew coconut trees mainly. The land was named *Tiger Cat*, after an animal that was spotted up in one of the trees. Pt Sirju invited a couple of young men from the village to pick the coconuts. Anant accompanied the boys in the boat as they headed out on their errand.

Anant noticed that the boys kept exchanging furtive smiles. Arriving at the plot, they proceeded to pick and fill the boat with the harvest of coconuts. Later, the boys revealed to Anant that they had gone to Tiger Cat earlier where they stole all the coconuts. This time with him in tow, they had actually stolen the coconuts from someone else's property! Anant had been none the wiser as it was the first visit he had made to the land. Guilt had made the men confide in Anant, they were too ashamed to admit it to his dad. A double whammy, Pt Sirju was never told the story; he would have confronted and lectured the boys, and insist that they admit their misdeed to the people from whom they had stolen.

Cricket Fan

Pt Sirju loved sports. In the days in Guyana before television, he would listen to boxing matches with the radio peeled to his ear. He had a special love for cricket, occasionally joining his sons when they played in the yard. He attended the local games played between villages, as well as national and international games.

Ravendra Kowlessar remembers seeing the 'big black umbrella' – that Pt Sirju often carried - moving down the road and would know that it was Pt Sirju walking through all the bad roads. When they were playing cricket at the school ground, Pt Sirju would quickly change from his dhoti and kurta and go to the ground to watch cricket if he did not have any other commitments.

Fatherhood, Family, and Grandchildren

Pt Sirju's grandsons Tishan, Jitin, Hardeep and Somant Maraj had made outstanding achievements in national and international cricket, providing their nana with much excitement and entertainment. The *West Indies Under 15* cricket team, with Tishan as captain, won the world championship award at Lord's in London, in the year 2000. Following that stretch, Tishan was captain of the *West Indies Under 17* cricket team in 2003 vying for the world cup when his team ended at the finals. Jitin, Hardeep and Somant played cricket at the national level in Trinidad and Tobago, winning much recognition and many awards.

Entertain His Children

To entertain his children when they were young, Pt Sirju would allow one or two to accompany him to a Kishore Kumar or Manna Dey concert, or a Vijayanthimala dance performance in Georgetown. These were major events in the lives of his children, and he drew immense pleasure in including the children in these entertaining, inspiring and educational opportunities.

In spite of a hectic schedule, he spent valuable moments with his children. He himself was curious, and to satisfy his own curiosity and also entertain his children meant the young family was treated to various events or sightseeing trips. These included visits to the museum, zoo or circus, or a trip across the newly built Mackenzie Road, or long drives to places of interest in Guyana, such as the Abary bridge. He took the family to see their first movie Sangam. Until his last days, he still loved it whenever the entire family accompanied him to an event. He was a true family man.

And while it was true that everyone was special in his eyes, and special treatment was meted out to all, it started with his own family. He was equally kind and considerate with each family member as with the people in his community. For example, whenever his family left on an errand and he had to close the door after them, he would smile and wave until they were out of sight. He would insist on taking the bus or a taxi home to not inconvenience his children; and he never forgot to say 'thank you' to his children for any kindness. When any of his family came home from the office or from running an errand, he asked how their day or their progress was. He offered little courtesies where he was totally engaged in his family's welfare, and he did not take anyone for granted.

Daughter Parbatee who lived with her dad and Dalia, said of her dad, that he was blessed with an "unassuming sweet and gentle nature." Noted for his meticulous record keeping, these included records of dates of major events in the lives of all of his children dating back to the nineteen fifties. Pt Sirju's family was dear to him, and he would have gone to the ends of the earth to make them happy.

Narendra Datt, Pt Sirju's nephew touched on one aspect of his uncle's love and care of the family: *He believed in the dignity of labour and no job was considered to be too menial for him when it came to providing for his family.*

The following message was delivered by a friend of one of Pt Sirju's children. The message captures the thoughts and impressions of his children. It offers a fitting summary of a father's gifts.

> *For those who knew him, they were for certain, privileged. How blessed is your family to have lived with and loved a man so caring and so kind. To lose a father, who has given so much of himself, lived peacefully and generously, and who loved his family so much brings unimaginable sorrow. Without a shadow of a doubt, you have a unique gift that a lot of people can only dream of; incredible, tender memories that will be with you, always.*
>
> *– Sylvie Falk*

Fatherhood, Family, and Grandchildren

Grandchildren

While growing up in Trinidad, Pt Sirju's four grandchildren Jitin, Dr Tishan, Hardeep and Somant Maraj, visited Canada very often, and as a result developed a close relationship with their nana. On one occasion, their father Dr Youtradeo Maraj was staying in Scotland for six months to prepare and write his surgical exams. His four boys and their mother Basso visited Pt Sirju and his family in Toronto and stayed with them for the entire period while their dad was away.

Pt Sirju and Dalia also visited often with Basso and her family in Trinidad. During the many visits, he and Basso's four boys could be heard having lively chats where they would be cracking up with laughter. For instance, the four boys found the choices to be much out of character, when their nana told them that during his youth, he thought of becoming a boxer or policeman!

Jitin, the eldest grandson, talked about Pt Sirju's message in the following eulogy he gave at the funeral parlour when the latter passed away:

> *This is by far the most challenging task I've been faced with, to see my Nana lying here in front of us, coming to the realization that I would never hear his voice again.*
>
> *Nana was a great lover of the Bhagavad Gita and I would like to start with a couple of quotes from this source.*
>
> *The first one goes:*
>
> *'For death is certain to one who is born; to one who is dead, birth is certain; therefore thou shalt not grieve for what is unavoidable.'*
>
> *And the second quote, which refers to the soul:*
>
> *'Never is he born, nor does he die at any time, he has never been brought into being, nor shall come hereafter, unborn, eternal, permanent and ancient. When the body is slain, he is not slain.'*
>
> *Nana was truly a great man, the epitome of all men. If there ever was a reincarnation of God to walk this planet,*

Nana was definitely one. I've never met a man with the wonderful qualities and principles he possessed. His outlook on life was godly, his humility, generosity, wisdom and ability to see the good in people cannot be matched.

He was a man that showed no prejudice to members of other religious backgrounds, creeds and race, he was truly a man of God.

Nana loved everyone around him. He treated all as if they were his children. His love was limitless and although we can argue that he had a full life of peace and personal fulfillment, in my mind, his life was much too short.

Nana has always preached to the grandchildren the importance of education and was always proud when we excelled. When I was much younger, living in Trinidad and vacationing in Canada, I remember he would always pull myself and my brother Tishan aside for random spelling tests and other questions. This may have been for learning as much as keeping us busy and out of mischief.

Even up to the 1st of January 2012, the last time I would have a conversation with him sitting comfortably on his favorite recliner in his living room, he still took a keen interest in my life, job and plans for the future. Nana preached to us about the importance of honesty, humility and keeping the right company. He also encouraged us to dream big, because without dreams, you would never achieve your goals. He wanted the best for us, and tried in his way to help us achieve this.

The more I reflect on the life of my late Nana, the more I see the impact he had on my life and the life of all the people around me.

To my mom, dad, brothers, uncles, aunts, cousins and darling wife, in this difficult time, we must reflect on the impact Nana had on our lives. Let us reflect on the impact he had on all these people sitting and standing in this building, and thank God that we were blessed with such a special, loving, caring and exceptional father and grandfather. There would only ever be one of him and we

Fatherhood, Family, and Grandchildren

were lucky enough to be close to him, and have him dear in our hearts.

They say behind every great man, there is a great woman and my Nani is a great woman. Being married for almost sixty five years, they have been each other's rock for the duration. I know nothing I say to Nani would comfort her at this time. But what I will say to Nani is that you must be proud of the way the two of you lived life together, be proud of what Nana has accomplished in his 88 years on this planet and to be strong and know that you have 10 loving children and 18 grandchildren including my wife Simi who love you tremendously and would do anything for you. I love you, We love you. Let us keep his memory alive and spread the messages he taught.

To everyone else, whether you are Hindu, Muslim, Christian, or don't believe in God, my Nana dedicated his life to ideal principles and actions. Although the root of his belief stemmed from Hinduism, we don't need to be Hindu to practise honesty, humility, compassion and peace. I think we all can learn a little from Nana as we leave here today. I know we may not be able to match his way of life, but if we can change ourselves just a little for the positive, his life lessons would have been fulfilled.

Nana, I love you, I miss you and hope that one day, someday, I may be privileged enough to speak with you again.

Thank you,
Jitin

Dr Tishan wrote the following memories of his nana:

Pt S P Misir was a gentle soul, beloved by all who knew him; a number which was reflected by the masses that came to pay their respects after his passing. He was my mother's father, or Nana, and I speak of him in his capacity as my grandfather.

As a child, there were 2 constants in the world - the sun rising every morning and Nana ringing his bell waking you up around 6 o'clock, during his daily morning worship. (This drove my brothers and me crazy, as we were usually on vacation.)

His enthusiasm for your achievements, regardless of tier, was contagious, giving you a sense of accomplishment and a boost of confidence every time you conversed with him. His ability to listen was incomparable and always without judgement. He gave advice that was immersed in spiritual knowledge, always relevant to your predicament, and you could be certain it was morally and ethically correct. When I was back in Trinidad, I could count on Nana offering his advice, best wishes and long distance blessing via telephone, especially when I was ill.

How a man in this day and age could lead his life rooted in dharma, unwavering from its path while keeping his entire, rather large family together and happy might be baffling to some, but to those around us, it was implicit. Dealing with his passing has been quite an ordeal for our family, and it is ironic that his presence and guidance would have allowed us to cope with such a situation.

Nana was truly a magnanimous individual whose counsel and way of life continue to inspire me daily. It is my hope that the same applies to those who were blessed with the good fortune of having some interaction with him and through this, his memory kept alive.

Hardeep had these stirring words about his nana:

Nana's passing has left us feeling incomplete. Sitting around the same living room we always do, an unmistakable absence is felt. A voice, a smile, a presence. However in a year where so much has changed, I would like to highlight all that stays the same.

For the past twenty four odd years that I've been on this earth, nana (and nani) haven't seemed to have aged a

> *day. Similarly as life changes, his presence was grounding, comforting and reassuring. Much as a pillar brings stability to a structure that is constantly evolving, he has been the one guiding the development of this family through the right path. The fact that the entire family can congregate at the drop of a dime is testament to the unit he has built. The accomplishments of his children and grandchildren are the fruit of his pursuit.*
>
> *He has shown us, sometimes through words, always through action, a model for life. He has demonstrated carrying yourself with pride, yet with humility; to be strong, yet gentle; the importance of knowledge, yet always being open to listen to another opinion. He has demonstrated how to be a good person, a good friend, a good husband, and a good father. Those lessons have been passed down to his children, grandchildren and all those who have been impacted by his life.*
>
> *When we remember, and practise these lessons that he has taught, it should be realized that the pillar he represented has not left; that which had been lain over decades is not as brittle as the physical body which represented it. His legacy endures, and will continue to be the example that allows me to stay grounded, seek comfort and refuge.*

Somant, the youngest of Basso's four boys recalled some of the memorable episodes in the brothers' relationship with Pt Sirju. Following is an excerpt from Somant on these memories:

> *Regardless of what we did in the day - school, cricket, music - it was the norm to sit and chat with nana on the front balcony in the afternoons before dinner. The balcony overlooked the sea and it was his favourite place to relax.*
>
> *We looked forward to these conversations, because nana was always engaged in what we were doing and asked insightful questions - specifics about a cricket tournament, what new ragas (g) I learnt in music class, and what do we want to be when we grow up. He had a way of getting us*

to talk most of the time while he just listened. As kids, this was not a problem for us, we could go on forever. As nana listened, he would smile and say how proud he was of us.

Nana was very sociable, he got along really well with complete strangers. He, along with other family members, attended presentations of the Trinidad & Tobago Cricket Under 15 awards, where I was among the honorees as part of the team. At the end of the presentation Nana made his way around the room, conversing with everyone. No one knew who he was, but he introduced himself, and observing from a distance, the conversations seemed hilarious with lots of smiles and laughs. Although I'm not quite sure what he said to the officials, later that day they told me that they met my grandfather and therefore knew a little bit more about me.

While growing up, we frequently visited Canada during summers and winters. On a number of occasions, nana invited me to accompany him to pujas. I was always excited to go because as a small kid, it was a chance to get some aarti cash. The main thing nana taught through just observing the way he lived, was to carry your person with dignity, but always be respectful and humble; and to be thankful for what you have and never forget where you came from.

With that said, it was always interesting to see nana in his true element and to see the way everyone treated him with respect as he entered their homes. This is truly something I would never forget.

Pt Sirju would often indulge his children and grandchildren on the lighter side with riddles such as *a herring and a half costs a penny and a half, what is the cost of one herring*, and *what is the oldest culture*. When they responded *Hindu culture*, he would say *got you. It is agriculture*. He teased his grandchildren mercilessly, touching their heads from behind, when they looked at him questioningly, he would say *wasn't me*. Kay's son Sachin told her recently that his nana was a lot of fun and he remembers how he used to pinch him playfully. Her daughter Divya said she wished her nana would come back.

Fatherhood, Family, and Grandchildren

Grandson Dhiren

Dhiren was 9 when his aja (g) Pt Sirju passed away. Dhiren wrote in an article, that ever since he knew aja, the latter would pinch him and give him spelling bees. He fondly remembers when himself, sister Tiya, and cousins Akshay and Shivaal would come to Aja's home and watch world wrestling - WWE - with him. He recalls aja visiting their home and smiling and laughing with them and having a good time at his aunt Basso's home. The speech he gave on his aja and aji's sixty first anniversary, when he was only five years old, may have been the shortest, but it was also complete. He said, *I love you very much.*

Short, but once again heartfelt, Dhiren's speech at the funeral parlour said: *We are all here for aja and here are some things he used to do with me. He would touch my hair and say it was not him and call me 'Sadhu' (g). I love him very much. Aja, I will miss you and never forget you.*

Shivaal, Akshay and Tiya

Shivaal, 13 and Akshay, 12 were always surprised how strong their aja was when he arm wrestled with them. As with his children and other grandchildren, they were not spared the spelling bees, and playful pinches. Instead of asking what their grades were, he would say, *so your grades are in the A's right?* He had much confidence in them and high expectations. Shivaal remarked that he would always hear aja chanting prayers as he walked around in the home. On one occasion when Shivaal was not feeling well, he remembers his aja praying over him and giving him a mantra to keep.

Tiya - Granddaughter

When Pt Sirju was in the hospital, Tiya had made a get well card for him. She gave the card to her dad, Hemant to take to the hospital but he forgot it at home. At the funeral parlour, Tiya said in her eulogy that she was upset when her dad forgot the card; but he had told her not to worry as he would give it to her aja the next day. She said that at the time, she thought to herself, 'what if there was no tomorrow?' Turning to the casket where her aja lay, she continued, *I didn't get to give it to you but will give it to you now*, then walked over to the casket and placed the card inside. The card read - *Get well soon Aja*. Tiya was 11.

Tasha and Dhanesh

Tasha and Dhanesh live in Queens New York. The two grandchildren, both in their twenties, accompanied their parents Anant and Radica each month to Toronto to attend the *shraadha* of their grandpa. The shraadha is a monthly prayer that is conducted for the duration of a year after the passing of a loved one. These are their memories of their grandpa:

> Tasha said - *I consider myself one of the luckiest grandchildren in the world. I have been able to call one of the greatest individuals my grandpa. Whenever there was a function, grandpa would be dressed 1ˢᵗ, sitting and waiting. When I asked him how I looked, he would say that I looked beautiful; to me he was a beautiful soul. Now that he is gone, a part of all of us is missing. I feel honored to carry on his values, morals and traditions. His legacy will be timeless and his memory will forever shine in our hearts.*

Dhanesh described some episodes that epitomised a few of his grandpa's qualities: *Along with my sister and a couple of cousins, I*

Fatherhood, Family, and Grandchildren

usually called him 'grandpa, not 'Aja'. It says a great deal that my Aja (aka my grandfather) didn't care. No one would've been surprised if he did mind, considering his standing as a well respected pandit and spiritual leader, yet the fact is he didn't. He never even mentioned it to us, because he understood what was important. He recognized that it wasn't the word, but the sentiment behind it that truly mattered. That is a very progressive manner of thinking, something indicative of the type of person he was. A pandit from Guyana in his eighties wouldn't seem likely to be a liberal individual, yet in many ways that's exactly what he was. He truly gave credence to the phrase 'never judge a book by its cover'.

The last time he came to New York, it was for a 3 session yajna my parents were performing. When Aja stayed in my room the first night after their arrival, I asked him which one of the suitcases was his. He didn't know how to describe the luggage to me, so I told him if I guessed correctly it meant I was supposed to be a pandit. He approved of my terms and waited as I chose a bag at random and brought it up to him. When I reached the room he smiled, telling me I was meant to be a pandit after all. I was surprised that I guessed correctly but I took it in stride. About ten minutes later he called me - it turned out it wasn't his bag at all! He opened it to find some women's sarees and various other garments he'd never wear.

He was so eager to tell me I was supposed to be a pandit that he didn't realize it was someone else's suitcase. Either that or he had no idea which was his - either way we all shared a good laugh about it, him included.

One day he was telling us that growing up he always wanted to be a boxer! When we laughed and asked him why he ended up conducting Pujas as opposed to sparring in the ring, he joked that he couldn't even win a fight against grandma - this would've explained the very different path he ended up taking. Afterwards, I sent him a pair of miniature boxing gloves imprinted with Guyana flags- he responded with great enthusiasm and hung them up in his office.

There was always more to him than what met the eye, and that episode stands out as a clear example.

Darsh - Grandson in Guyana

Darsh, a grandson who lives in Guyana with his mom Chandra and dad Yudishthir, enjoyed a close relationship with Pt Sirju whenever the latter visited Guyana. Darsh wrote these words about his memories of Pt Sirju, his nana:

> *I was privileged and blessed to be in nana's company and to have known him, he was what I would declare a once in a lifetime individual, a truly remarkable man.*
>
> *Nana was the pinnacle of simplicity and kind heartedness. He was a role model and a child's dream for a grandfather. His smile reflecting a gracious personality charmed the hearts of all those who dealt with him.*
>
> *Whenever he visited Guyana, I got the opportunity to spend long periods of time with him. These moments gave me a chance to pick up invaluable spiritual guidance and catch up on all affairs. Nana's selfless service to the community continued, even though he left the Guyanese shores many moons ago. Whenever he came back to Guyana he went on his marathon walks between Dochfour to Greenfield visiting almost every home offering kind and inspirational words.*
>
> *Nana was always interested in my plans for the future, and would offer career options that he thought would be best suited for me. I often felt awed by the strength of the personal power that radiated from him.*
>
> *His hallmark feature was a never ending smile. Regardless of the situation, no one has ever seen my Nana, Pandit Sirju Persaud Misir angry. He carried that smile reminiscent of his character, until he had his last breath.*

Pt Sirju related to each age group. He had the ability to be childlike when he was among children. Pt Sirju maintained a close and loving relationship with all of his grandchildren.

Fatherhood, Family, and Grandchildren

Brother-in-law Pt Inderpaul Tiwari – Touch the Heart.

Pt Inderpaul, Dalia's brother, lives in Guyana. He selected the following poem, author unknown, to describe his brother-in-law Pt Sirju because he said that the poem described the spirit of his brother-in-law, his attitudes, and how he lived, a rare soul.

Touch the Heart
Touch the heart with a smile
That sends a welcoming message
Dispatch a bouquet of flowers
Which exudes sweet fragrance
Give an amicable embrace
That emanates warmth and affection
Send a touching card
That expresses gratitude and appreciation
Make a phone call to say how much you care
And in your silent moments
Convey good wishes and pure feelings
With the power of your thought
Touch the heart
And experience a Happy Heart

Pt Inderpaul reflected on the different ways that his brother-in-law Pt Sirju encouraged and supported him on his journey as a Hindu priest. As he was getting ready to read his first yajna, Pt Sirju mentored him on prayers and topics for his lectures. He said that Pt Sirju was a patient listener who encouraged and enlightened him. Pt Sirju was more than a Guru, he always shared and was very simple and humble. Not only was he there to instruct him, but Pt Sirju also added the little touches, fixing his shawl and phagri, and a spray of cologne, before setting him up on the singhasan podium. He stated that these were some of the touching and meaningful gestures that resonated and inspired him. Pt Sirju's guidance prepared him to conduct many yajnas since his first.

Pt Inderpaul claimed Pt Sirju's life was devoted to giving of himself. He always smiled no matter how difficult a situation he was faced with. Therefore, he reminded him of the poem, Touch the Heart.

Yudhisthir Rampersaud – Son-in-law

Yudhisthir is the husband of Pt Sirju's daughter Chandra, they live in Guyana. His story captures the spirit of the total, unhurried presence with which Pt Sirju embraced each encounter.

In the 1990's, Pt Sirju and Dalia were on one of their many visits to Guyana from their home in Canada. During these visits he would normally pay courtesy calls on old acquaintances. Although he did not carry a gift, I know he carried a practical message. It was a weekday around 2:30 pm and I was working in the store. Panditji came downstairs, peered through a window of the store and enquired as to what time my wife Chandra would be home. She was a teacher at the nearby Anns Grove Community High School. I explained that classes would normally be dismissed at 3:00 pm and teachers are expected to remain an extra half hour for administrative duties. He then disclosed that he would like to visit a friend at Mahaicony, about eight miles from Clonbrook.

I was fully cognizant of Panditji's many standard time-consuming visits, so I quickly gathered and deposited reading materials in the aged car – a Victor Vauxhall. We started on our way to Mahaicony around 3:45pm. There were few cars on the road during that era. While driving, we passed an occasional car, numerous cyclists, pedestrians and a few donkey carts. Along the way, the road was lined with flowering plants and trees laden with their special variety of seasonal fruits. There was the usual diverse range of dilapidated and new houses. Eventually, Panditji pointed out the home we were going to. A huge mango tree at the edge of

Fatherhood, Family, and Grandchildren

the fence promised a cool shelter from the hot sun, and I parked close by avoiding the fallen fruits. When we arrived, as usual, Panditji invited me in but I declined. He would have a lot to catch up with his host, and I planned to settle in with the reading material I had brought.

Eventually, I took a break from reading and my thoughts centered on a reflection of Panditji's qualities as a human being – a warm and congenial personality with pious resonance. After some time, I became uncomfortable and instinctively glanced at my watch – time was moving rapidly and the sun was receding further into the distance. The old car was working reasonably, but both Panditji and I knew that the headlights were out of order. I thought if I reversed the car towards the gateway, it would send a message to indicate that I had changed position and time was up. The doorway to the home now became my singular focus.

I started to become very apprehensive. Some of the options occupying my thoughts included buying a torch to light the path home, or driving behind another vehicle with lights; or better yet, reaching home before the sun set. I waited with increasing impatience for my passenger to appear. After a while, I gave up hope and reluctantly stopped staring at the doorway. I now began to gaze at inconsequential objects that met my eyes. Suddenly my attention was directed back to the doorway. As if by magic, Panditji emerged, idled a few moments on the porch, and started to negotiate the steps. Unbelievably, he made a sudden turnaround and disappeared back into the home. I was dumfounded. I gave up, nothing mattered any longer. The dying sun now dominated my thoughts.

I was taken aback when suddenly Panditji appeared a few minutes later, standing at the gate. He quickly entered the car and innocently asked whether he kept me too long. Without looking him in the eye, I blatantly lied by replying in the negative.

From Mahaicony to Mahaica, a four mile stretch, the road was quiet. I pressed on the gas pedal. Both of us were aware of the distance and this time, there were none of the usual comments from him about speeding. Climbing over the Mahaica bridge, I could see the setting sun. As a sort of consolation, we had by now arrived at relatively safe territory

Living with Purpose

in terms of proximity to home, and, better visibility on the roads. All the while, Panditji seemed to be unconcerned, but I knew in my heart that he was offering a silent prayer to the Sun God for our safety.

Teasingly, the sun seemed to stay at a standstill for a while. Miracles do occur. As soon as we arrived at the Anns Grove bridge leading into Clonbrook, the benevolent sun disappeared. We reached home in utter safety. As we entered the yard, a couple who had been waiting for Panditji, greeted him with 'SeetaRam'. He responded brightly, as if he had just stepped down after a rejuvenating rest from upstairs. I simply hurried up into the home for a little breather, exhausted by the worry over the lack of car lights.

Now Panditji has gone to the beyond; while he lived, his inclination was to go on working as hard as one can to clear as wide a patch of efficiency, good will, cultural contribution and constructive endeavour as possible; in the hope of making the world a slightly better place. May his soul rest in eternal peace.

Dalia

Pt Sirju, in response to a supposed difficulty would often say - *I leave it in the hands of Lord Krishna*. A deep abiding faith in God, coupled with unconditional support from Dalia sustained him when times were tough, and allowed him to follow his dreams. His life partner Dalia, supported him in all his ventures, including any assistance Pt Sirju wished to provide to others.

Pt Sirju and Dalia would have celebrated their sixty fifth wedding anniversary one month after he passed away. At the age of eighty five, the two of them related in an interview conducted by Adit Kumar, a writer for the Indo Caribbean World that living together for sixty one years was a matter of sharing, love and understanding. Adit Kumar stated ... *At 85, Panditji displays a sharp mind and lots of wit. Panditji has a lot of wisdom to pass on to people of all ages. He advises to do good, keep good company, be good to your parents and elders and*

Fatherhood, Family, and Grandchildren

do not forget your Dharma or culture. Both he and his wife said that love and understanding were responsible for keeping their marriage together for so long and they would like to pass this advice on to all. They both said that - ups and downs will be there but good understanding is paramount to a successful marriage.

During the early years of their marriage, when they were very poor, no one would have guessed that they barely had enough to make ends meet because they never complained. Dalia's mother, Gangadai, often remarked to Dalia's children that her daughter Dalia never once complained about her life. Gangadai on relating this observation, seemed awed at her daughter's composure and self-reliance.

The immediate neighbourhood in which Pt Sirju and Dalia lived, was not a quiet one by any standards. There was always a commotion going on, with neighbours yelling and screaming at one another across fences. Pt Sirju's home was one of the few in the neighborhood where there was never a voice raised in anger between Pt Sirju and Dalia. Occasionally, voices were raised between the parents and their children, but neighbours commented that they never heard a raised voice between Pt Sirju and Dalia, or between Dalia and any of her neighbours. Dalia and Pt Sirju created a home where respect and care for one other and for each member of the family was the cardinal principle.

Chameli, Pt Sirju's mother, lived with her son and Dalia until she passed away. In all, Dalia lived with her mother-in-law for about twenty one years. Chameli was a vibrant, hardworking lady. She spent most of her time manning the grocery business or she helped Dalia with small household tasks in the kitchen. She loved her grandchildren and spoiled them with discriminating affection and a love that overflowed. She pronounced that the grandchildren were too delicate to be bothered with 'menial' household chores so she completed the chores for them in order to free them up to read or play!

Dalia enjoyed a great relationship with her mother in law for all the years together. Even if her mother in law fretted about anything, Dalia stayed quiet. They never spoke a harsh word to each other in all the years they lived together. Dalia has a truly amazing thoughtful quality. This quality is likely what allowed her to complement Pt Sirju so perfectly.

Dalia was the 'money manager' in the family. Pt Sirju always handed over all of his earnings to Dalia. He said that she managed it so well and that he could never do as good a job as she did. She not only managed the family's personal finances, but all of the cash from the store was her responsibility as well. Dalia in turn, never objected to any of Pt Sirju's enterprises including those for which he needed cash from her. Whether it was helping an individual or a charitable organization, she supported him.

Dalia's day started at 5 am. She prepared breakfast for her family, which consisted of her husband, his mother, and Dalia and Pt Sirju's ten children. Dalia then prepared and packed lunches for each child to take to school. Once they had all left, she spent her day between completing household chores, and helping out at the grocery business. By the time her children had all returned from school at the end of the day, dinner was ready.

After dinner Dalia would have some time to engage in one of her hobbies such as gardening. Her flower garden included a large variety of multicolored hibiscus, and a host of other flowering plants such as coxcombs, jasmine, croton, and ladies slippers. Her other hobbies included flower arrangement, home decorations, cooking and baking.

She also liked to spend time with her immediate family. This included her parents, siblings and extended family. Attending family events were a must for Dalia, and Pt Sirju always accompanied her to these events. Dalia would often spend weekends with her mother and family whenever they celebrated major events such as weddings.

Dalia also managed all affairs related to picking the fruits and vegetables from their land. The extensive farmland provided

Fatherhood, Family, and Grandchildren

Pt Sirju's family and the villagers with a large selection of fresh fruits and vegetables. Dalia organized with vendors to purchase the produce. Both Dalia and Pt Sirju collaborated in taking care of the trees and plants in the yard.

In addition, Dalia was not one to have her children sit idly by while their parents labored. She wanted them to learn that discipline and hard work offered their own rewards. Dalia successfully delegated tasks related to cleaning the home and yard to each of her children.

Pt Sirju was a caring partner to Dalia. Whenever she did not feel well, Pt Sirju would go to any lengths to help her get better, just as he would take care of his children. Dalia did the same for him. Dalia often suffered from disruptive sleep patterns. At these times, if Pt Sirju saw that she was taking a nap during the day, he would keep the phone close by so that she would not be disturbed if it rang.

As Narindra Datt, Pt Sirju's nephew described Dalia's devotion to Pt Sirju as: - *He had a Dharampatni who lovingly and dutifully supported him for sixty five years and enabled him to achieve his full potential.*

As a life partner, Dalia was a perfect complement to Pt Sirju. Pt Sirju was an extrovert while Dalia was an introvert. She worked at home, planning and managing family activities, and running the home; while Pt Sirju worked mainly outside. Pt Sirju loved to be with his family, but he also enjoyed social interactions outside of the home. They made a perfect team, and Pt Sirju always said that Dalia deserved life's best.

Living with Purpose

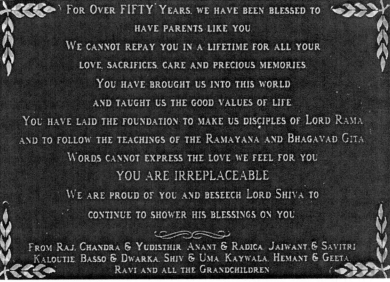

50th Anniversary Plaque from children and their families

CHAPTER 9

Friendships

Show me your friends and I'll show you who you are...
Words of Wisdom, Confucius

The chapter delves into some of the friendships that Pt Sirju cultivated to illustrate the nature and depth of these relationships.

Bhawan Friendship

Bhawan was a successful businessman who, like Pt Sirju, started off from poor beginnings. Like Pt Sirju, he too left school at a very early age. Through a combination of hard work and an ingenuity that seemed to spring from genius, Bhawan created through his company - the Shiva Woodworking Establishment - a singular brand of furniture products for the home.

The company began humbly enough. Working alone from the ground floor of his home, Bhawan began creating furniture pieces to supply a niche market for home furniture such as dressers, tables and chairs to local residents. Dalia recalled that Bhawan built the first dresser that her family owned. It needed to be delivered to their home, but Bhawan did not own a vehicle, therefore he and an assistant fetched the furniture to her home by boat!

From the finely honed craftsmanship in the pieces he constructed, it soon became evident that he possessed a rare creative talent. It didn't take long for the locals to recognize Bhawan's gift. As his cleverness and reputation for quality products quickly spread, the orders for products increased at a rapid pace.

The Shiva Woodworking Establishment developed steadily, and eventually expanded to include a large complex housing the latest technologies and employing many. Located at the industrial site in Enmore on the East Coast of Demerara, the company supplied the country, and exports to other countries, a wide range of high quality household furniture products.

Bhawan and Pt Sirju shared the same values – moral, family, and spiritual. The two men were both self taught, they had strong family ties, and a strong sense of community spirit. Like Pt Sirju, Bhawan was a teacher and role model for his family, friends and acquaintances.

Starting from these early years, the two developed a close relationship. They sought each other's counsel on matters relating to community activities as well as on personal challenges and choices. However, the discussions between the two never reached the intensity it did, as when it turned to an examination of the Vedic texts and its meaning and lessons for humanity. These discussions went on during any and all occasions when the two friends met. They visited each other's homes frequently, and the conversations picked up as if they had never left off.

P.P.Shivraj, son-in-law to Pt Sirju's eldest brother Seecharan, remembers these discussions and the impressions they created in his life:

> *On many occasions when I visited his (Pt Sirju's) home in Clonbrook, I would see people coming to him for counselling and guidance on matters ranging from domestic problems, to matters affecting the community at large. They would*

> *return home very satisfied with the advice and explanation given them.*
>
> *Then there were others like Mr. Bhawan Singh's and Mr. Raghunandan's episodes, these gentlemen would come to discuss the scriptures, the Mahabharat, Ramayan etc. As a young man in my twenties at the time, I was very impressed with these discussions and arguments put forward and viewed them as constructive, harmonious and worth emulating.*
>
> *No doubt, these discussions must have created an impression upon me to read our scriptures as well as to learn the Hindi language. This I did intermittently between my very demanding schedules, studying for the ACCA examinations and playing cricket.*

Bhawan's was the kind of company that Pt Sirju kept, for he was someone like himself, who was searching for answers. The nature of the dialogue between Pt Sirju and his close associates such as Bhawan, created lasting impressions, and coloured the experiences of individuals such as Shivraj and many others, including Pt Sirju's own children.

Religious Discourses

The discussions between Pt Sirju and Bhawan covered all aspects of the Hindu religion ranging from the caste system to specific events described in the texts. The men's interpretations concerning significance of the events were covered in their entirety.

One such discussion centered around the well-known story of Droopati and how the Kauravas (g) tried to shame her. In this story, Droopati is brought before the Court where all the powerful Kauravas including Duryodhana are gathered in Duhsasana's Court. Then one of Duhsasana's men, in his attempt to humiliate the Pandavas (g2), attempts to undress Droopati by pulling at her sari.

Sitting in the audience was the venerable Bhishma Pitama, revered by both the Kauravas and Pandavas. One would have expected the honorable Bhishma Pitama to intervene on behalf of honour. However, he was a friend to Duhsasana, and therefore sat silent through the indignity about to be carried out on Droopati.

The scriptures describe how later during the Mahabharat (g) war, Bhishma Pitama was suspended on a bed of arrows for many hours after being wounded. As Krishna was passing by at the end of the war, Bhishma Pitama cried out to him, asking why he was suffering so terribly. Krishna reminded him of his participation (albeit passive) in the humiliation of Droopati.

As a result, the discussion concluded that Bhishma Pitama's suffering at the time of death was a lesson. Although he was an intelligent person, he acted wrongly in allowing his friendship with Duhsasana and the Kaurava clan to cloud his judgement. These discussions were thrilling to listen to, and many a visitor to the family of Panditji or Bhawan were treated to the intellectual commentary concerning the teachings in the Hindu holy books.

Religious discourses between Pt Sirju and Bhawan went on well into the night. Their debates in Pt Sirju's living room would often wake the family members sleeping in the adjoining bedrooms. The dialogue often grew more heated as the night progressed.

The topic of murtis (g) and accusations of 'idol worship' was a common theme in the discussions between Pt Sirju and Bhawan. Like all Hindus, they looked on the murtis as a means to help in focusing on a form (of God). The Arya Samaj movement was a breakout faction of the Hindu religion that occurred in the nineteenth century. The founder, Swami Dayananda Saraswati a Hindu by birth, questioned some of the prevailing Hindu beliefs and customs. Not the least of these was the use of murtis in religious events. The rishis (g) and swamis in Hindu chronicles who had achieved God realisation did not need visual aids such as murtis to pray and meditate. They were able to visualize and pray to God without the use of the murti. This was viewed as a sign of ultimate enlightenment.

Pt Sirju and Bhawan were often engaged with village followers of the Arya Samaj movement, in the debates to explain the Hindu rationale - for use of murtis, and for the differences that separated the two factions. Following the debates, the two friends often spent many more hours in post analysis as they revisited and evaluated both sides of the arguments.

In the following episode, Bhawan is describing to Pt Sirju, his exchange with an Arya Samaj follower.

Bhawan to Pt Sirju: *The Samaji (g) says that the Ramayana is not accurate. I asked him to show me the part of the text he was questioning. He returned later in the day to my workshop carrying the Ramayana. I was not impressed that he would rush over with the book and in anger and passion, hope to win a discussion; and reminded him that one must have reverence for all sacred texts, handle with love, and only then can one attain a greater understanding of all things.*

The story provides an example of the nature of some of the religious dialogues that occurred in the village community and how the two men supported each other in their reasoning and religious quest.

The discussions between Pt Sirju and Bhawan typically carried on with an intensity that disregarded constraints of time or minor physical discomforts of hunger or fatigue.

One afternoon, Pt Sirju was on his way home to Clonbrook from the city of Georgetown. He alerted the driver – Rampi, his son-in-law - that he wanted to stop at Bhawan's place along the way. There was an ensuing discussion in the vehicle between Pt Sirju and his son Shiv who was not happy about having to make the stop, as he was tired. He knew that his dad's visit with Bhawan would not be a brief one.

As they got closer to Bhawan's place, Shiv engaged his dad in a conversation as an attempt to divert him from his intention to pull over at his friend's place. As they approached Bhawan's premises, Pt

Sirju broke off from the conversation with Shiv to warn Rampi that, "remember you have to stop." They agreed that the best thing would be to drop Pt Sirju off at Bhawan's, and continue on home. Bhawan would take him home after their discussions. Pt Sirju repeated to Shiv and Rampi that he was going to be at Bhawan's for only a few minutes, but in actuality he did not return home until the early hours the next morning.

Bhawan - Electricity

In 1959, when Pt Sirju read his first seven day yajna in Clonbrook to open its new temple, the villagers did not have any electricity. Coleman gas lamps and candles provided lighting for the homes. To provide lighting for the yajna, Bhawan loaned an electric generator to the temple. At the time, Bhawan was highly indebted, owing a considerable debt borrowed with interest from a money-lender. He still saw it within his power and ability to provide help at no cost to the temple.

Like Pt Sirju, Bhawan was dedicated to God and to his religion. Soon after the yajna was completed, Bhawan became extremely ill. Pt Sirju visited every day to pray and offer tulsi-water (a medicinal herb), until his friend made a full recovery.

More than ten years before electricity became widely available to the region through Government sources, Bhawan's home and ground floor business had electric power. He was also able to provide Pt Sirju's home with electric power from his generator; the cable wires ran across two long streets and two trenches to reach Pt Sirju's home! In his turn, Pt Sirju was a loyal friend. He supported his friend unconditionally.

Bhawan had negotiated a deal with a wealthy landowner to purchase a parcel of land. The landowner accepted an advance towards purchase of the land, but later refused to honour the agreement. Bhawan discussed the options available to him with Pt Sirju, who offered to approach the landowner on his friend's behalf.

Pt Sirju was a skilled negotiator, with an ability to appreciate and examine all sides of a position. The famous line from the Ramayan, *praan jaye par vachan na jayi* - life may go but words should be kept – a line that he often used, finally convinced the landowner to honor the deal with Bhawan. The land provided the site where Bhawan eventually established his Shiva Woodworking company.

Test of Friendship

One day, another Hindu priest dropped in to visit Bhawan at his workshop. Bhawan knew that the priest was a very good friend of Pt Sirju. However, Bhawan, fiercely loyal in his friendship with Pt Sirju, wanted to put the visiting priest's friendship with Pt Sirju to a test. The test was to malign Pt Sirju to get the priest's reaction. The priest did not fall for the trick, he passed the test in flying colors by disagreeing with Bhawan's comments.

When Pt Sirju was preparing to leave Guyana in 1982 to come to Canada, he went to Bhawan's to bid him goodbye. They hugged, and Bhawan said to him, *you're leaving your brother*. Pt Sirju visited Guyana several times after that, never failing to visit Bhawan on each occasion. At these meetings, the discourses would continue as if they had never stopped.

The two friends Pt Sirju and Bhawan maintained their close association until the end. When Bhawan passed away in 1992, Pt Sirju travelled to Guyana to pay his last respects and conduct the funeral rites of his friend. The funeral was done in accordance with the Hindu scriptures as his friend Bhawan - a stickler for adherence to the rites as prescribed in the Vedic texts - would have wished.

Pt Sirju and Bhawan Singh shared a friendship that was beautiful and strong and based on loyalty, and a discriminating sense of what was good and right. It was a friendship of two people who saw life as a cherished gift, one to be taken advantage of at all levels. As Julius Erving, noted American athlete discovered, *the key to success is to keep growing in all areas of life – mental, emotional, spiritual, as well as physical.*

Corbin's Story

Those who frequented Pt Sirju's home for counselling included individuals of African ancestry from the surrounding villages. Corbin, a prominent African businessman from the neighbouring Anns Grove was among those who, before he undertook any business venture, often sought Pt Sirju's advice.

The devout lifestyle of the Hindu people in the community epitomised by Pt Sirju intrigued Corbin. Corbin had started a new business in the village in the mid nineteen sixties, but before opening the venture to the public, he invited Pt Sirju to offer a prayer. It was an example of the deep-seated trust he held for the advice that Pt Sirju provided.

Corbin kept in close touch with Pt Sirju and the two developed a close friendship. A story of the cow belonging to Pt Sirju underscored the close relationship between the two friends.

The cowherd was guiding his animal flock home after the day's grazing at the pasture. One of the animals strayed off the path and rammed into an oncoming car. The cow suffered small injuries, while the car received some damages. The driver of the vehicle guided the animal to the neighbouring police station. At the station, he filed a complaint against the owner, and asked help from the police to identify the owner, in order to recover costs for damages to his vehicle. At the station, the animal was immediately tied up.

The cow was identified as one that belonged to Pt Sirju. As word got to the villagers that one of Pt Sirju's cows was hurt and impounded, a crowd took to running to the Police Station to investigate. This caused the policeman to observe loudly, "It is only the man's cow that is hurt, what if something happened to the man himself!"

Corbin's son Michael - the driver of the vehicle - and his family, on learning the identity of the cow's owner, asked the police to release the cow. They declined any monetary compensation from Pt Sirju, and additionally, Michael was sent by his mother to apologise to Pt Sirju for the inconvenience caused by involving the police.

The cow was released from the police station. She stopped 'bawling' and rushed to suckle her newly born calf. The calf, deprived of its evening milk feeding had been in the throes of loud agonised wailing, immediately quietened at its mother's arrival.

Judge Kissoon

Pt Sirju was a major influence in the lives of the Kissoon brothers. He took the youths under his wings in study of the Hindu texts and guidance on the teachings of the faith. Over and above his interest in their religious upbringing, Pt Sirju showed a continuing interest and provided positive feedback in their professional development.

Prabhudyal Beepatnath, a Christian priest from the village related this story concerning one of the Kissoon boys:

> *My good friend and judge Nandram Kissoon who loved and respected Pt Sirju dearly, once told me that Pt Sirju went to the courthouse to visit him while the court was in session. Nandram immediately got up from his chamber and bowed at Pt Sirju's feet. Some in the courts were amused. Nandram's response was that he held Pt Sirju in high esteem as a guru, and he was the person who taught him a lot on Sanatan Dharma for which he was forever thankful.*

Other Friendships

Pt Sirju befriended everyone who happened to cross his path.

A few years before his passing, sitting in the waiting room at a hospital in Toronto, he was waiting for Dalia to complete her medical tests. He soon started a conversation with the elderly lady sitting at the next chair. The lady, it turned out, came from the same village where Pt Sirju grew up. She was a close family friend to the DaSilva's who had taken care of Pt Sirju as a little boy. The fortuitous encounter allowed Pt Sirju to get in touch with George DaSilva's sister-in-law, Marie, who lived in Las Vegas. Marie visited Pt Sirju in Canada soon after he spoke with her. She passed away in 2011. Before she did, Pt Sirju's children wanted to know what their dad was like as a young boy. Marie's memory was that even at a young age, he was a responsible, serious lad who felt he needed to take care of and protect his family, which consisted at the time, of his mother and siblings.

On one occasion, when Pt Sirju was chatting away incessantly with someone sitting beside him at the doctor's office, his daughter asked whether the person was someone he knew before. Not surprisingly, he answered that they just met. This was a regular occurrence in his life. At the local Bank where he did his regular banking, he greeted everyone. The lady banker, after enquiring whether his hair was real, remarked that he must have been a really handsome young man.

Ramnarine Singh, like Pt Sirju, was in his mid-eighties and the two of them attended the Vishnu Mandir, through which they became friends. Ramnarine, whenever he was alone, called Pt Sirju regularly. They spoke for long periods many times a week. When Ramnarine complained of not feeling well, Pt Sirju offered a prayer over the phone.

In a time of extreme problems and sicknesses, Pt Sirju was the type of friend one was grateful to have.

Friendships

Harold Kowlessar captured the close relationship his dad Basil and their family enjoyed with Pt Sirju. Basil passed away in 1979 at age fifty nine, but his children, including Harold, continued to demonstrate a wonderful fatherly love towards Pt Sirju. The following is Harold's description:

> *I recall Pt Sirju used to ride a 'big frame' bicycle, which was often parked in his yard. As kids, we would always try to steal a ride. It was a regular routine to visit his home from time to time and to be treated with tasty refreshments. He would visit our home often - I mean a whole lot. These times were special to us kids to literally see and feel the love which exuded between him and my parents. Even if we had to go without, my mother always seemed to have fresh milk tucked away somewhere as a treat reserved for him, to be served in his special glass.*
>
> *On his regular sojourn in and out of the village to perform functions as a Priest, we would watch for him because we knew he would be bringing us a treat of prasad, other goodies, and yes, a few pennies. Never did I see him pass our house without a hand wave or some such gesture of acknowledgement. We always looked forward to him doing Hanuman Swami jhandis at our home. From childhood, I still fondly recall his favourite bhajans which were always uplifting. This was the only time my dad would give up his 'Berbice chair' to someone else. It was not unusual for those two to be talking in riddles and cracking up with laughter..their secret jokes no doubt. He did have a great sense of humour.*
>
> *One evening I recall he came over to discuss a life insurance policy with my dad. Even though it may have been tough to keep up the premiums, I heard my dad say he could not bring himself to decline his best friend so he must find a way. Pandit Ji had a special wooden briefcase which my brothers and I always jockeyed as to which one of us would be honored to carry for him on his way home.*

Loved by Elderly and Kids Alike

He was greatly loved, admired and respected by people from all walks of life, especially the elderly and little children of Guyana. He was equally approachable to the very young or very old; to the frail, the healthy, and especially so to anyone who needed a friend. Not only would he not desert anyone at their time of need, but he would face the situation together with the person as if it was his own problem.

His many friends extended beyond the barriers of race or religion. It is difficult to capture the names of all those who spent many hours with him on a regular basis. No matter if they were Hindus, Muslims, Christians, blacks, Caucasians or Indians and other races from the village, his relationship with each was special.

Pt Sirju often quoted these words from Swami Vivekananda:

> *I accept all the religions that were in the past and worship with them all; I worship God with everyone of them; in whatever form they worship him. I shall go to the mosque of the Mohammedan; I shall enter the Christian Church and kneel before the Crucifix; I shall enter the Buddhist temple...I shall go into the forest and sit down in meditation with the Hindu, who is trying to see the light ....*

It was the creed by which he chose to live.

Long Walk

The 'car park' as it was known, was really a multi-purpose section of the thoroughfare. At this juncture, the four roads leading from the villages of Anns Grove, Clonbrook, Dochfour, and Bee Hive converged with the main road leading from the public road into the village. As a result of the confluence of people, the area was a hub of activity in the early mornings when it served as a market. Here, vendors sold their produce until about 7:30 am when the market phase wrapped up and the area turned into a car park.

It was the late nineteen seventies, and many individuals in the village earned a living driving taxis and minibuses. As the market activity was wrapping up, the drivers would start arriving to line up their vehicles awaiting passengers to begin their daily commutes. Many students and workers relied on taxis for transportation, so that on a normal morning, it could take many hours before one could end up getting a ride.

On one of these mornings, Pt Sirju was preparing to travel to Georgetown on business. His daughter Parbatee was also getting ready to leave for classes at the University of Guyana. As Pt Sirju's car was at the mechanic's, Parbatee and her dad headed out together to the car park. The road to the car park lead to the neighbouring villages of Bee Hive and Greenfield and was busy with people from each village going about on their morning errands. As they started the what should have been a ten minute walk, Parbatee said that her dad not only stopped to greet everyone, but had a conversation with each person as well. He was genuinely interested in everyone's welfare and what they had to say. They too were eager to engage him, and the conversations flowed smoothly.

Parbatee recalled that she was becoming impatient and irritable as she had a class to attend. She asked him why a greeting was not enough and he responded that people are *'not inanimate objects like sticks'*. She said that as they dallied, she could see that the park was very busy and many were awaiting transportation, further increasing her anxiety about getting to class on time. As they neared the park, a few of the taxi drivers greeted her dad and inquired where he was going. Her dad seemed to be in a predicament on how to choose one of the drivers without hurting the others. He took up the first offer and explained to the others that this one had motioned him to his vehicle first, and he thanked them anyway. Parbatee said that after the experience, she joked with her father that she would not walk out with him to the car park again.

> *Be grateful for whoever comes, because each has been sent as a guide from beyond.*
>
> – Rumi

Friendships

Pt Sirju at 83

Chapter 10

Leaving Guyana; Canada Days

Autumn is a second spring when every leaf is a flower.
— Albert Camus

To date, Pt Sirju had embarked on a lifelong course of self education and learning that started from a very early age. The manner included creative, sometimes unorthodox, ways of getting at the information that he was looking for. An example of this is when he invited a learned visitor to the country from India to stay at his home. Pt Sirju hoped to have crammed sessions with the visitor so he could learn as much as possible from him over the course of the visit, but the visitor only imparted information at his own slow, steady pace.

Beyond unusual means such as this, Pt Sirju educated himself through the various traditional ways - taking courses through the Guyana Pandits Council, reading extensively, attending lectures, and discussing and mentoring with the learned. Through the different methods, he had amassed an immense amount of information. His ease and enthusiasm in picking up new material, was matched with an equal readiness to share it.

At the age of twenty three he became a Hindu priest. At the time, his community Clonbrook was in dire need of a leader to guide them through changing tides, and he was a natural choice to assume the role. He had all the qualities of a leader – integrity, intelligence, dedication, love of people, and a determination to make things better for all. As he took on the new roles, he immediately garnered respect and influence with the people in the community. He was not only a dynamic preacher of the profound teachings of the Hindu philosophies, but he was also trying to live the ideals they espoused.

To parents, he preached the importance of a good education for their children. As a parent himself, he made sure that his own children were given all the opportunities for a sound education. He tutored young children on Hindi, and bhajan singing, but his main emphasis rested on passing on the core values as he saw them - education, morality and a greater purpose to life. He encouraged the children to utilise their talents and develop various skills. He wrote speeches for his young students, encouraging them to present to the temple audiences and develop their public speaking skills. He encouraged others to chant and sing bhajans to large audiences. These were means to engage young minds in the understanding of the religion, while at the same time, helping them to develop various skill sets.

Pt Sirju was a friend of people of all ages. Children, as well as the elderly loved him. He had a way of making each person that he interacted with feel that they were the only one who mattered at that moment. He was a leader who guided his community with soft speech and a quick smile, but with a deep spiritual conviction. On par with his spiritual leadership, he was an indefatigable social worker and teacher. But there came a time when he knew he needed to leave his beloved community in Guyana and emigrate to Canada. On his leaving Guyana, it was said that - *the light had moved away from the community.*

Pt Sirju left Guyana for Canada in the summer of 1982. The reasons for the move were manifold. Guyana, during this period in its history, was experiencing many pressures on all its citizens. Peoples of all races and religions felt that progress in the country had not only halted in each of the areas of economy, culture and education, but the political instability had reached a new low. Freedom of speech and movement was restricted. Shortages of rice and sugar, both produced locally, and in some cases, a ban on basic, imported food materials were the norm. Being caught with these banned products, could result in jail sentences. The oppressive environment forced many to leave their beloved homeland, to seek better opportunities abroad for themselves and their children.

Before the nineteen seventies, the University of Guyana was still in its infancy, offering no major professional programs, having first opened its doors in 1963. During this period, emigration from Guyana took the form of students going abroad to pursue education in law, medicine, nursing, business and other professions. The majority headed to England, Canada, and the United States. Students pursuing law and nursing went to England, while those looking for a career in medicine went to Canada, US, India, the University of the West Indies in Jamaica, or they went on scholarships to Cuba or Russia offered by the Guyana Government. Canada and the US were also popular destinations for careers in business and education.

Following the phase of student emigration, the next major wave of emigration from Guyana started in the mid 1970's. Entire families uprooted and left the country in waves. Canada's liberal immigration policy brought many to that land, others moved to the USA, seeking better opportunities than those they had left behind. Many families from Pt Sirju's communities were among those who left, and many more had plans to follow suit. Pt Sirju was receiving requests from those already in Canada to move to that country. His decision to leave for Canada was made after careful thought, including the prospects for his children's future.

Before he left for Canada in 1982, he made sure Clonbrook's spiritual community would be taken care of by his son Jaiwant, who took on the priestly duties. Three years later, Pt Jaiwant prepared to migrate to the United States. Pt Sirju, once again, expressed concern that his beloved people in Clonbrook and nearby villages would be left without a Hindu priest.

He went to Annandale to meet with Pt Laikram Tiwari, telling him that he was not comfortable that the villagers would be left without a Pandit to conduct their ceremonies. Pt Laikram agreed to help by accepting Pt Sirju's invitation to visit Clonbrook to meet some of the residents. Pt Sirju spent two days with Pt Laikram walking him through the village street by street to meet with the residents. The people emerged from their homes to greet him, so he used the opportunity to introduce and recommend Pt Laikram. Everyone invited them back to their homes where they were offered refreshments.

Following these introductions, Pt Laikram started to perform pujas for almost everyone in the village.

Pt Sirju felt that he had a responsibility to the people of his village he had left behind. He wanted them to continue in their journey in which he had hitherto been a large part of, even when he no longer resided in their country.

Pt Laikram later moved to Toronto. In Toronto, Pt Sirju also recommended him to yajmans in Canada. When attending functions with Pt Sirju, Pt Laikram said that he was always asked to take part either in the havan (g) ceremony or to offer a prayer.

Ottawa Days

Pt Sirju carried his light with him when he arrived in Ottawa, Canada in 1982 at the age of fifty nine. He left Guyana with a powerful and moving legacy behind. Many of those who knew him have observed that - *Pt Sirju came with a Mission*. In Ottawa, he started to conduct pujas, and soon after presided at a yajna in that city.

In addition to the religious services, Pt Sirju's services to the community included counselling couples with marital issues, or helping families to resolve differences. He offered prayers over the phone for the sick, offered quotes from religious texts and explained the relevance of these teachings to their lives. He spent many long hours with families of bereaved, as he sang bhajans, and read selected verses from the Hindu epics to console the bereaved.

He advised families who sought advice on prayers and rites to be performed during sickness, or when a member was deceased. He also advised and blessed young children, or assisted young priests with instructions and prayers. He also offered these instructions to anyone who was interested in acquiring the prayers. If there was a newborn in the family, the parents often asked him to consult the patra to determine planetary conditions under which the baby was born, and provide a suitable name for the child. When asked, he checked the gana, or compatibility of bride and groom, to provide auspicious dates for wedding, religious functions and successful business ventures.

In all areas of his life, Pt Sirju espoused the notion that it was a privilege to have this human birth. Each moment counted, and he believed that to procrastinate would be to waste that precious moment. One of his first actions on arrival in Canada was to apply for the Certificate of Registration that authorized him to solemnize marriages in the province of Ontario. He obtained the certification soon after, in the same year of his arrival. With this designation, he performed countless marriages in Ottawa and Toronto.

Final Prayers, Ottawa

Pt Sirju had been the priest for a family in Ottawa whose patriarch was terminally ill. At the hospital, the doctors had given up on the elderly man in his seventies. The family, who had already made funeral arrangements as the doctors had given the man only a few hours to live, called Pt Sirju to offer final prayers. Pt Sirju arrived at the man's bedside at the hospital, and started to chant prayers from the Bhagavad Gita. After he had finished chanting, the man's condition started to gradually improve. The doctors were at a loss to explain the sudden changes in the man's condition. The family, mystified, praised Pt Sirju for saving the life of their loved one who went on to live for another seven years.

Pt Sirju's son, Pt Jaiwant, remembers that on the many occasions such as this when anyone praised his dad for remarkable accomplishments, his dad would quote a verse from the Ramayana. Translated, the verse stated that all things acquired or accomplished comes from God. Pt Sirju was a humble man, and could not take any credit for what he knew was God's will.

Security Job in Ottawa

When Pt Sirju first moved from Guyana to Ottawa, he missed the many interactions that he was accustomed to having with the people in his homeland. He thought it would be interesting to find a job that allowed him to get out more often, and soon after found a job at a security company, where he worked for a few months.

The company had recently fired Shiv, Pt Sirju's son, for sleeping on the job. Shiv had been working the night shifts as a security guard in a building that housed the partially blind. One night, there was smoke in the building but Shiv was nowhere to be found. The management eventually found him sleeping comfortably in a room with the door closed. They fired him on the spot.

When the company hired Pt Sirju, they warned that he could not fall asleep like the previous guy. Pt Sirju found humour in that they were actually referring to his son. The family had tried to discourage Pt Sirju from taking the job as he had already worked hard in his life but he was insistent. No job was too menial for him to do.

He did not merely survive the job, but relished it. He looked forward to all conversations and interactions with the residents. He enjoyed writing reports at the end of his shifts, a task most people would find to be tedious, but not Pt Sirju. He found creative ways of saying the same thing, calling the night 'serene' or 'tranquil' or 'calm.' Most often he called up his children for their assistance in conjuring up words that could be used to describe a 'calm' night so that his report could be made a bit more interesting for the reader. He had a childlike quality in savouring each of life's adventures.

During the period of employment with the security company, Pt Sirju found out that there was an opening for another security guard. It was the early nineteen eighties, and jobs were difficult to come by in Ottawa at the time. His children were all attending school on a full time basis, but were eager to supplement their stipend with part-time work. Pt Sirju passed on the information to his son Hemant, who was soon hired. On his first day at the job, Hemant received a pleasant surprise when he learnt that his dad would be training him. Pt Sirju, the eternal professional, showed him around and directed him on his responsibilities.

Inspiration From Nature

Pt Sirju drew inspiration from nature. He would sit outdoors for hours on a summer day watching the flowers, birds and other animals. One peaceful summer morning, about three hundred birds had gathered in the huge empty field behind his home. He excitedly called out to his family to look out to witness the birds in their assembly. He spent a long time watching as they moved about in orderly droves, and joked that they were likely having a meeting, and wondered what was being discussed. Nature had a fascination with him.

He enjoyed frequent visits to the Experimental farm, a 400-hectare (1,055 acres) expanse of historic, and cultural heritage land established in 1886 as a research station in the centre of Ottawa. The farm, administered by the Ministry of Agriculture, supported many research programs affecting plant and animal behaviour and modifications.

At the farm, he made a beeline for the station that showcased the large, gleaming Holstein cows. The cows were specially bred and were beautiful to look at. The research staff explained that each cow would produce over four times the amount of milk that an average cow produced! Pt Sirju loved to look at the cows and hear the stories told about them. He visited the farm often, mainly to look at these animals, even though there were many other interesting sections to visit. The animals likely brought back childhood memories of him milking and tending to his own cows.

Moving to Toronto

In 1988, Pt Sirju moved with his family to Toronto to take advantage of the better job opportunities available for his children in the larger city. A large Hindu community was based in Toronto. It included people from the West Indies as well as from countries such as Fiji, India, and Africa. A large segment of the Hindu community from Guyana had migrated to Toronto; therefore Pt Sirju had often traveled from Ottawa to Toronto to perform pujas. Pt Eshwar Doobay, a chela of Pt Sirju, related that his eldest brother was one of those who invited Pt Sirju to officiate at a puja at his home in Toronto. Pt Eshwar stated that his family could have chosen a local priest in Toronto, but wanted Pt Sirju to conduct their puja, as they had much affection for him and had appointed Pt Sirju as their family priest since the nineteen fifties. He and four siblings were Pt Sirju's chelas. Pt Sirju made a profound, indelible impression on him, including a sense of how to conduct his life.

Upon moving there, Pt Sirju was very much at home in the city where he was called upon by this large group to perform religious and community services. He also became a regular attendee at the Vishnu Mandir in Richmond Hill.

Pt. Bhoj Sharma is a priest at the Vishnu Mandir, Richmond Hill, where Pt Sirju was a patron. He and Pt Sirju's relationship dates back many decades and he described their association as:

> *I have known Pt Sirju for about 45 years as a practicing pandit and have performed many poojas and weddings alongside him in Guyana and in Canada. He was one in thousands and will always be in my memory as someone who holds no malice or hate. He was simple, humble, and always encouraged upcoming pundits to higher education in pursuit of the teachings of sanatan dharma.*
>
> *Pt Sirju's name, fame, smile, and loving disposition was evident in the thousands who paid tribute to him at the wake in Vishnu Mandir and the funeral home. His soul is undoubtedly one with the divine.*

Wherever Pt Sirju lived, people came to him for guidance. He continued to offer counselling, reassurance and mentoring in Toronto similar to as he had done in Ottawa and Guyana. One such benefactor was Shanti Edun. She had known Pt Sirju since 1989 when he had just relocated to Toronto from Ottawa. She lived a few minutes walk from his home, and recommended many couples who were having marital issues to him. They included individuals from religious denominations other than Hindus.

Shanti stated that her daughter was three and son five years old when a relative passed away. Following the death, the children were having nightmares and could not sleep. She discussed the problem with Pt Sirju, who gave her a prayer for the children, after which they slept peacefully. She said that Pt Sirju had a healing touch.

When her father was hospitalized, she came to Pt Sirju, who after consulting with the patra, told her that her father was near death. He advised her to go to the hospital and whisper a prayer into his ear. She said that her father took his last breath about five minutes after she completed the prayer.

She has seen Pt Sirju bless kids who were not focusing on school by holding their heads, praying and blessing them. She indicated that she had referred many individuals— Hindus, Muslims and Christians— to Pt Sirju and he helped all. So much so that they would inquire about his well being and thank him.

Jayt

Living in Toronto, a stone's throw from Pt Sirju, Jayt Jugmohan was entering high school when he started to accompany Pt Sirju to religious events. A young lad of fourteen, he diligently attended all functions such as pujas and weddings with the priest for a period of about five years until the rigors of a university program required more of his time.

Jayt described his experiences during the period spent with Pt Sirju:

> *In the early part of my life, religion played a major role which helped to shape me into the person that I am today. These joyous and educational memories were in part the result of a very influential person – "Big Pandit." We affectionately referred to him as Big Pandit since he was one of the oldest, most respected priests known to our family. He was always willing to provide guidance to any individuals seeking help or who had questions.*
>
> *In growing up, I was eager to learn more about our religion and since our families shared a close relationship in both Guyana and Canada, I began to accompany him to religious ceremonies. As a young boy, this was an incredible opportunity as he was highly knowledgeable in the Hindu community. There were countless times while performing pujas; where he would take the time to stop and explain to me and the audience the underlying meaning of the steps being taken. He would always try to ensure that I was retaining the procedures by asking me questions and*

> *ensuring that I had written copies of prayers in order for me to follow along and memorize. At that time, I was attending Indian musical classes to learn to play the harmonium and sing; and he always tried to allow me a chance to sing bhajans as a way of motivating me and allowing me to practice what I had learnt.*
>
> *One of the key teachings from him, which I still practice today, is the steps in performing a Hawan (puja). It is needless to say that his teachings have remained with me throughout the years, and will be passed on. He was an exceptional individual and I will always be appreciative of the knowledge that he bestowed upon me.*

Another Toronto resident, Dolly Panday, remembered Pt Sirju fondly. Dolly Panday was having an annual puja at her home, with Pt Sirju officiating. Her niece's son, a two year old, sat beside Pt Sirju. As the rituals were being performed, where offerings of fruits and sweetmeats were being made to God, the child started to cry. He said that he was hungry and wanted the banana that was being offered as part of the oblations.

Dolly said that Pt Sirju picked up the banana and gave it to the child saying *Beta (g), eat this,* while commenting that the child was like a little angel, a God sitting among them. The child ate the banana and not only did he stop crying but he sat attentive throughout the entire puja.

The child continued to sit beside Pt Sirju during pujas for the many years following. The kid never seemed to forget Pt Sirju's act of kindness. Dolly attributed the child's comfort to Pt Sirju's gentleness, and the soft manner in which he addressed the child. Dolly said that after each of the many pujas Pt Sirju conducted, she felt an immense peace that pervaded the entire home - the effect of prayers offered with love.

Guiding Priests

Pt Sirju provided prayers and mantras he had in his possession to anyone who needed them. Some Pandits came to him for instruction in selecting appropriate prayers for specific events. He enjoyed these opportunities, and never felt insecure about sharing his knowledge.

Pt Ramnarine Tiwari felt that because Pt Sirju was so guileless and honest, he was one of the very few people with whom he felt comfortable enough to ask for guidance. He stated that Pt Sirju was a mentor who was not envious of anyone; he was honest, unselfish, soft, helpful and always willing to share his knowledge.

Pt Sirju explained and added clarity to any of his questions, which he supported with quotes from specific sections of the scriptural texts, all from memory. He said that, wherever he went, Pt Sirju lit up the room.

Pt Sirju did not mind if someone other than he was selected to preside at a function. To the contrary, he was happy when someone else was given an opportunity to make their contribution; as he thought that every person had something unique to offer. He was eager to listen to what each one had to say. Many attested to this extraordinary quality that he possessed - one which recognised the unique and divine spark within each individual.

Lifetime Learner-India Trip

Pt Sirju held a deep seated interest and fascination with India, the land of his forebears. When invited by his son-in-law, Dr. Youtradeo Maraj, to join him on a tour of that country in the year 1995, he accepted the offer with much anticipation. Dr Maraj's father Parmanand Maraj and chacha (g) Tribhuwandat Maraj would make up the rest of the tour group. Dr. Maraj had lived and travelled widely in India while a student studying medicine in Bombay. He was the perfect tour guide for the three older men - all in their early seventies – because he was knowledgeable in the older men's shared interest of every expression of the mythical and cultural artefacts in the mother country he understood well.

Pt Sirju, as a matter of course, documented the details of their journey in his daily journal, neatly labelled for his records. Some of the highlights are reproduced here, describing his impressions of places and facets of the culture that he experienced.

Arriving in New Delhi, they visited the Raj Ghat, a black marble platform with an eternal flame burning. A memorial to Mahatma Gandhi, it marks the spot of his cremation which took place in 1948. Pt Sirju had always held an intense interest in the life and works of Gandhi. He was heavily influenced by the Mahatma, especially on his philosophy of non violence. He often quoted Gandhi's "an eye for an eye only ends up making the whole world blind." Pt Sirju's early book collections in Guyana included Gandhi's works on *The Story of My Experiments with Truth*, and the Mahatma's autobiography. At the Raj Ghat, everything that he had read about the icon flashed across his mind. Here he was actually standing in the midst of a plethora of history that so far he was only able to read about from afar. He felt blessed at this moment. Not only for this experience, but for the ecstasy he felt in visiting the land of his ancestors.

The objects of their stop the next day at Varanasi, a one hour flight from New Delhi, were no less historic. At the first, the birthplace of Buddha just outside Varanasi, the pillars of the original palace in which Buddha was born in 567 BC. still stood. Although all the structures around the palace were in a state of broken down ruins, Pt Sirju wrote that the aura of the great soul lingered on.

The city of Varanasi is located on the banks of the Ganges in Uttar Pradesh and is considered to be the holiest city in India. Some Hindus believe that death at Varanasi brings salvation. The Ganges is also the most sacred river to Hindus and is worshipped as the Goddess Ganga in Hinduism. From where the pure clear spring starts at the foot of the Himalayas to this point at Varanasi, a couple hundred miles, the Ganges is also a lifeline to millions of Indians who live along its course and depend on it for their daily needs. Pt Sirju and his two older companions had planned on a 'holy dip' in the waters of the Ganges, but arriving at the river banks, they seemed aghast at the murky conditions of the water in the fabled river.

A boat ride of a few hundred yards took them from the ghats – sites used for bathing and cremation that lined the western banks—to the clearer eastern banks where they partook in a dip. Pt Sirju's serene expression in the picture praying in the Ganges reflects his reverence for the holy river. It was early morning and the water was very cold, but he seemed oblivious, even with pants rolled up to above the knees, and legs exposed.

Pt Sirju was captivated by the large number of Buddhist and Hindu temples that this city alone contributed. He was equally fascinated with the elaborate architectural designs and the different causes that many of the temples advocated. One of these so called 'special' temples that they visited included the Bharat Mata temple. The name translates to "Mother India" and the followers of this temple pray for India to re-unite with Pakistan, to revert to the India as it existed before partition!

A principal objective of Pt Sirju's visit to India was to visit the places of worship and spirituality for which the country was renowned. Here in Varanasi, his wish was already fulfilled by the rich number and beauty of its temples that lent the country its reputation.

They devoted the next day for leisure, to savour and reflect on the absorbing expeditions in India so far, and spend the time as each saw fit. Pt Sirju opted to stay in the vicinity of the hotel area to relish the exotic sights and sounds of the city. As he headed out through the hotel lobby onto the street, he spotted the scene where some monkeys were entertaining a crowd that had gathered. With their handlers beating damru drums, the monkeys performed dance movements to match the changing rhythm of the drum beats. He was so enthralled with the spectacle, that he wanted everyone to see it, and rushed back up onto their fourth floor rooms in the hotel and got his son-in-law to come down and take pictures!

After Varanasi, the next stop was in Bombay, followed by Bangalore. At Bangalore, they visited the Shri Sathya Sai Baba Ashram. Shri Sathya Sai is an Indian guru, he passed away in 2011, but still leaves millions of followers all around the globe, including in Canada and the US.

They continued on to the city of Mysore about 91 miles southwest of the capital Bangalore. Mysore is noted for its palaces and for the festivities that take place during the Dasara festival - a royal festival celebrating victory of truth over evil - when the city receives a large number of tourists. In Mysore, they visited the Emperor Maharaja palace and the beautiful temple on top of the Chamundi Hills. The hills rise to a height of 3,489 feet and are visible at a distance when travelling towards Mysore. They stopped at the magnificent Vrindavan Gardens which attract close to two million tourists annually. The visit at the gardens was one of their more memorable experiences. About a mile in length, the garden was exquisitely laid out and featured a unique array of plants and ornamental features. The long walk from one end of the garden to the next did not seem to tire Pt Sirju and his two older companions. Too engrossed in the beauty surrounding them to notice fatigue, they pondered on the paradox of the poverty they saw in India, versus the abundance and prosperity of places they had seen - such as this garden. Pt Sirju noted that they had left the hotel at 7:00 a.m. that day and had not returned back until 11:00 p.m. They were on the road for sixteen hours, but Pt Sirju's love of learning fuelled his energy on this trip.

In Madras the following day, they visited more temples and Pt Sirju noted that they saw a mango tree that recorded 3,500 years. Its branches were said to yield four different types of mangoes. Pt Sirju was touched with all that he was experiencing in these travels. He wrote in his journal, *we saw where Rajiv Gandhi was killed, rice planting, ploughing and various crops, the ocean, temples on hills and other loving things.*

They returned back to Delhi and after visiting more places of interest, travelled to Mathura, Vrindavan – land where Lord Krishna was born and spent his youth—then to Agra. While on this leg of the journey, their progress was interrupted with a vehicle malfunction when the fan belt on the car broke. While the driver went into the city to get a replacement, the group waited by the roadside for a few hours. They weren't troubled by the fan belt problem. Pt Sirju, Parmanand and Tribhuwandat, like little children were more interested in their new surroundings, in this case a wheat field beside the road which differed from the rice fields that they were familiar with. Their tour guide had to keep them from walking into the field, where trespassing was not looked upon with favour.

On their way to Jaipur the next morning, they were treated to an unusual sight of big black bears performing tricks along the road side. Pt Sirju was mesmerised watching the animals performing their various feats in tune with the music, including dancing on two legs. Hindu mythology features the various animals including bears, monkeys, snakes, elephants and of course cows. The legends explain the absorption of Pt Sirju and the group with the antics of all the animals that they encountered.

Jaipur is known as the *pink city* of India because the colour of the stone used in construction of all the structures is pink in colour. In 1876, the Prince of Wales and Queen Elizabeth the second visited India on a tour. Maharaja Ram Singh chose pink as it denotes the colour of hospitality and the whole city was painted pink to welcome the guests.

In Jaipur, the temple at the top of a hill attracted the attention of the group. Reaching the temple required riding on the back of an elephant. Pt Sirju declined to go for the ride, stating that he couldn't have fun on the "back of an animal." Pt Sirju noted in his journal that they continued with sightseeing in Jaipur. He listed the beautiful Mansingh palace, but as always, never failed to observe and list the animals that they encountered - camels, monkeys, and elephants.

The next day, after an early start, they headed for the city of Rishikesh before returning to their starting point of New Delhi. Rishikesh, sometimes nicknamed *the world capital of Yoga*, as the name describes, has numerous yoga centres that attract tourists. Such tourists included the Beatles, who lived and composed many songs here. John Lennon also recorded while at Rishikesh. Rishikesh is a peaceful city with innumerable connections to Hindu mythology. Old brick temples and large ancient peepal trees provide the perfect friendly hang-out for the monkeys that scamper and engage the visitors mischievously. They all give Rishikesh the far-away look of something too idyllic to be of today's world. No alcohol, meat or fish is allowed into the region, epitomising the Hindu ideal of austerity. Pt Sirju enjoyed the serene beauty of this environment. It captured his imagination of a perfect setting for one seeking peace through meditation.

The group arrived back at the hotel at 8.00 pm to relax for the next, and last day tour in New Delhi. In New Delhi, they enjoyed a rickshaw ride through the city. That was a fitting way to enjoy the sights of the city at a leisurely pace, and a perfect way to end the trip. Pt Sirju made his last purchase in New Delhi, a 100 year old patra. They left Delhi on March 16, 1995 to journey back home – Pt Sirju to Toronto, Parmanand and his brother Tribhuwandat to New York, and Dr Maraj to Trinidad. Pt Sirju's dream of a life time was fulfilled: a religious and cultural odyssey. The visit - in addition to the enthralling, indigenous artefacts and sceneries each region showcased - provided insights into the mysticism and customs that Pt Sirju's ancestors brought from their homeland, many of which he had adopted.

Music, Lectures

Music was one of Pt Sirju's passions. He attended all classical and religious performances that came to his attention. Some of these included the Misra brothers - Rajan and Sajan Misra- classical singing at Vishnu Mandir, Anup Jalota and Manna Dey concerts. Listening to bhajans was integrated as a part of his daily routine, which included his morning prayers and exercises.

Anant Rambachan is a professor, author and religious scholar living and teaching in Minnesota, USA. Anant, originally from Trinidad, studied at the University of the West Indies, Trinidad, following at University of Leeds and then at a Hindu seminary in Mumbai. Pt Sirju attended the last yajna Anant read at the Vishnu Mandir in 1992, and was so impressed by Anant that he bought a copy of all the tapes of the yajna that were being sold to raise funds for the Vishnu Mandir.

There was always a book at his night table, and an interesting book or article would inevitably be passed along to family or friends as highly recommended reading. Pt Sirju continued with exhaustive study and reading until the end. He had extended his reading to include notable western authors such as Joel Osteen, Dr Wayne Dyer, and Eckhart Tolle among others.

He bought books and magazines from Leela Hansraj, KC Sharda, Leela Persaud, Pt Ishri Maraj, Pt Somdatt, and Vishnu Mandir. He also subscribed to Sanathana Sarathi, the monthly magazine of Sathya Sai Organization which was published by the Sri Sathya Sai Books and Publications Trust, India. The magazine provided spiritual knowledge with an objective to uplift humanity mentally, morally and physically. His yearning for knowledge and upliftment never ceased.

One of the items he took with him to the hospital during his final hours was Swami Jyotirmayananda's 'The Glory of Lord Krishna, Mysticism of Srimad Bhagavatam' which describes the exploits of Lord Krishna (g), together with the mystic explanations behind the stories. Then, two days before a massive heart attack called him away, his request to his children was to bring him a copy of Joel Osteen's *Your Best Life Now*. It was a book that he had already read; yet reading spiritual texts remained a priority to him until his last days.

Other's Views of Him

Pt Sirju had an impact on so many people, it's difficult to convey all of their stories, but here are a few.

Ravi Sharma was a chela of Pt Sirju. He was the grandson of Sew Singh, who with his brother Jog Singh were closely connected with Pt Sirju. He was their family priest since the early nineteen fifties. The Singh family had lived in Enmore Guyana, before migrating to Toronto.

Ravi related that on a day in the year 2003, he came across Pt Sirju at the passport office in Scarborough, Toronto where the latter had gone to renew his passport. Pt Sirju enquired after Ravi's nani's health, as he had known that she was not well. When told that she was in the hospital, Pt Sirju said that he wanted to visit her.

After they were both finished with their business at the passport office, Ravi drove Pt Sirju to the hospital. They were allowed in after Ravi told the nurses that Pt Sirju was the family priest. Ravi's nani was very happy to see Pt Sirju, who then proceeded to offer prayers. Even with the tubes in her mouth, they could see her lips moving in prayer.

Ravi's cousin was only forty three years old when he collapsed and succumbed to a heart attack. Pt Sirju was one of the large gathering who attended the funeral. Ravi was quick to mention that Panditji attended even though he was not the officiating pandit. He recalled that Pt Sirju had gotten a ride to the funeral parlour, and upon seeing him walk across the parking lot, Ravi held on to his elbow as a guide as they proceeded together into the room.

All the seats in the room were filled with people standing along the aisles at the two sides and at the back of the room. Ravi said that as he was walking Pt Sirju through the crowd, everyone wanted to reach out and touch him; they were greeting him with *Seeta Ram Panditji*. He said that while ordinarily, one could not get through such a crowd, it was easy to walk through because of Panditji. Most of the people in the room came from the village of Enmore in Guyana. They knew who he was, and made way as they saw him approaching. Ravi said he led Panditji to the front of the coffin where he offered a prayer.

Ravi concluded these memories with - *I would do anything for this great soul.*

Sattebhama Doodnauth, a long time chela of Pt Sirju, related that she often had long conversations with her health care provider. During one of these discussions, Dr. Mehta was interested in knowing who her guru was. Dr. Mehta was acquainted with Pt Sirju through their common affiliation to the Vishnu Mandir. He remarked that she had made a good choice of Pt Sirju as her spiritual guide. Sattebhama stated that in her eyes, her guru was exceptional and his presence always exuded divinity. He brought light even in darkness.

One of his chelas of forty years, Pt Sukhdeo Maharaj, recalled the last interaction with his guru. The meeting occurred at a yajna sponsored by his guru's son Anant and family in October 2011, in New York. Pt Sukhdeo and his family had gone to the yajna one evening. As his two young children were sleepy and tired, he did not stay for the meal afterwards.

Later that evening, he received a phone call from Pt Sirju's son Pt Jaiwant who mentioned that his dad was looking for Pt Sukhdeo after the yajna so that they could have dinner together. Pt Sirju seemed appeased after Pt Sukhdeo promised that he would try to attend Sunday morning after completing a puja he was slated to perform.

Following his wife's persuasion that the family should attend as they never knew if it could be the last time to see their guru, Pt Sukhdeo arranged to have his puja done earlier by explaining to the people that his Guru had come all the way from Canada. Pt Sukhdeo was able to have what turned out to be the last meal with his Guru. The love and devotion was reciprocated between a Guru and his chela.

Pt Sukhdeo recollected that his guru was always considerate. Whenever Pt Sukhdeo called, his guru did not want to engage him in long conversations that could be expensive. Pt Sukhdeo would reassure him that it was not expensive, as he had a long distance plan. They talked often after the meeting at the yajna and Pt Sirju would enquire whether he needed copies of various prayers or if he already had them. The Guru wanted to leave his chela with all the tools he needed to perform his job.

Udal Singh lived in the neighbouring village of Bee Hive, a few minutes walk from Pt Sirju's home in Clonbrook. He and Pt Sirju shared a close relationship which continued when he moved to Toronto with his family. In Toronto, they continued the relationship which included long conversations over the phone.

Udal was hospitalized in a Toronto hospital during the same period that Pt Sirju was admitted to the hospital where he passed away. Udal's grandson, Umesh Singh, related that the family tried to protect his grandfather from the news that Pt Sirju had passed on, as they did not want to upset him while he was sick at the hospital. It seemed that he got hold of the news somehow, as he was constantly inquiring from his hospital bed about Pandit, asking whether it was true that he had passed away. Udal was devastated when he eventually found out and he passed on one week after Pt Sirju.

Umesh, Udal's grandson, also had a long personal connection with Pt Sirju. He said that he was just about seven to eight years old when the connection started. Pt Sirju would pass by his home on his way from conducting his pujas. Whenever he saw Pt Sirju coming, he would run out to the road to meet him, to talk to him and get some mohan bhog. Pt Sirju would stop, inquire how he and the family were, rub Umesh's head as a token of affection, reach into his bag and with his soft voice would say, "look I brought this gift for you ok?" He gave him whatever sweets he had. After a while Pt Sirju found out that he liked pera (g) so he would try to save it and give it to Umesh. Umesh declared that Pt Sirju was an exceptional human being who lived a truly wonderful life. He was so well respected by people. Umesh knew him as a part of their family.

Umesh, who is a successful businessman in Toronto, owns a couple of jewellery stores, for which he designs and crafts his own gold merchandise. His hobby is music, he owns and leads a musical band which performs at community events. Besides the great nurturing influences of his own family – his mother, nani and nana – kind words from role models such as Pt Sirju no doubt made a positive impact in the lives of youths such as Umesh.

Raghnauth Singh, a devoted chela of Pt Sirju reminisced on the many spiritual discussions he had with his Guru. Raghnauth maintained a very close relationship with Pt Sirju and drove him to many functions. Ragnauth knew the type of religious hymns Pt Sirju loved to listen to. He had a large and varied selection in his vehicle which he played for his guru. Pt Sirju often compared the selection of music his children listened to, with Raghnauth's. While his children may include pop with their religious collection, Raghnauth's selection comprised of only the religious. Pt Sirju often remarked to his children that he wished they would follow Ragnauth's example in the choice of inspirational bhajans that he maintained in his repertoire.

Ragnauth described that in one of their discussions, his guru told him that in order to free this body from the cycle of birth and death, one has to get rid of the enemies of man - lust, greed, anger, pride, jealousy, hatred and delusion. His guru also stressed on the importance of being honest and truthful. This was also a typical conversation Pt Sirju conducted with all of his chelas, his children and grandchildren.

Raghnauth joined the five sons of Pt Sirju to perform the monthly shraadha for the duration of the entire year after Pt Sirju's passing.

Dhaman Kissoon, Barrister & Solicitor in Toronto, and originally from Clonbrook shared these thoughts:

> Pandjit Sirju Persaud was a giant of man. He was no ordinary man. When others needed many small steps to cover a certain journey he covered it in a few leaps and bounds. His journey was long but sustained. Panditji officiated in the marriage ceremony of my parents in 1952. Over the next fifty years he performed many pujas and religious functions for our extended family. This did not happen by accident. He was the choice because he was respected and because he was very knowledgeable.
>
> My first meeting with Panditji was at the Clonbrook Hindu temple when I was a little boy. I remembered him chanting for hours without referring to any text or religious book. I was simply amazed. I remembered him telling me you have to read when I asked him how he remembered so much. I initially wanted to follow in his footsteps to become a priest. That did not happen, but he did create opportunities for myself and others to follow him. We were allowed to accompany him as he journeyed from village to village conducting pujas. Not only did we learn from him, but he also gave us an opportunity to earn a small stipend. His kindness and generosity has remained with me indelibly. He was a role model for us.
>
> As I became older and understood the dynamics of the village, I realized that Panditji was the glue that held it together. He was not only present in times of celebration, joy and laughter but he was also present during times of sorrow and pain. That was the true sign of a leader.
>
> Every journey begins with a single step and it ends in the same manner. The success of some journeys is measured by the distance travelled, while others are calibrated by the impact the traveler had in the lives of the bystanders. By every measure or calculation Pt Sirju's journey was a very successful one. He has left the world a better place and his footprints are firmly planted in the sands. This was a giant of a man who soared above and beyond ordinary men.

Last Days

Pt Sirju's memory and mental abilities remained fully intact until the very end. However, as age was catching up, he started to reduce the number of pujas, referring yajmans to young pandits. He started to do this long before he passed on. At the yajman's insistence, he maintained only a very few for whom he continued to conduct pujas.

Pt Rabindranauth and Laikram Tiwari were among the young pandits to whom Pt Sirju started to refer his yajmans. Pt Rabindranauth stated that Pt Sirju had a special ability to help reconcile differing opinions to bring people together.

One month before he passed away, Pt Sirju performed his last puja at Balram Brijmongal's home in Toronto. Balram was a yajman for whom Pt Sirju often conducted religious functions. Balram said that it became clear to him that Pt Sirju was in tune with his future. He said that when Pt Sirju presented him with a summarized version of the Bhagavad Gita, a tranquil expression came upon Pt Sirju's face. It was the soothing expression of a fulfilled being accompanied with a long drawn-out smile. Balram said that not only was this a mesmerizing moment, it was one he would always cherish dearly.

Pt Sirju attended his last funeral just a few weeks before he passed away. His son Hemant had taken him to the funeral parlour and Pt Sirju was called to the podium to offer his contribution. Hemant recalled that there were two individuals standing behind him and they were saying how good Pt Sirju looked and were trying to guess his age. At the age of eighty eight, Pt Sirju was still attending funerals and praying for the deceased.

Pt Sirju loved life. He believed that each moment was given to us to be relished, to be used in service - service to oneself, to humanity, and to God.

> Service to oneself – be the best you can.
> Service to humanity – help as much as you can.
> Service to God – remember him always.

Pt Sirju preached the great teachings of Hinduism and spirituality, but more powerful than his preaching was the way he lived his life. His kind gesture, soft spoken words, and quick laugh created a unifying force for everyone around him.

> *Everything in the universe is within you. Ask all from yourself.*
>
> – Rumi

Praying at the Ganges

Epilogue

The famous sloka from the Bhagavad Gita of Lord Krishna's injunctions to Arjuna was often quoted by our dear father in many congregations. As we contemplate our loss, these words seem to be more poignant than they ever did.

> *The soul never takes birth and never dies at any time nor does it come into being again when the body is created. The soul is birthless, eternal, imperishable and timeless and is never destroyed when the body is destroyed. Just as a man giving up old worn out garments accepts other new apparel, in the same way the embodied soul giving up old and worn out bodies verily accepts new bodies.*
> *~ Bhagavad Gita, Chapter 2 -*

In his last year, the family observed many signs that our father was preparing to leave the physical world. He prayed for longer periods and was often lost in meditation. He made phone calls to individuals with whom he had not spoken to in years. He was gradually withdrawing from mundane affairs and he was regularly seen lost in thought. Did he have a premonition? Was there a knowing, a foreboding, that caused him to relate and relive the story of his father's passing just weeks before his demise?

At 9:30 p.m. on his last night at home, our dad prevailed in familiarizing Parbatee with the pertinent family documents he had filed away. He uncharacteristically emptied his citizenship and other cards, bank book and keys onto the dresser. Our father habitually listened to the Lord Krishna bhajan before going to sleep, but near the end, he played it louder with each passing night. Requesting Parbatee to remove the plastic wrap on the Bhaj Govindam compact disc, he watched with a smile as she proceeded to play the new song. It was the last night he spent at home, and he was surrendering to the Lord. The translation of the first line of the bhajan is - *Adore the Lord, adore the Lord, adore the Lord Oh fool! When the appointed time for departure comes, the repetition of rules will not, indeed, save you.*

The inspirational notes and quotes discovered in our dad's room after his passing included Ch 2 v 13 from the Bhagavad Gita, spoken by Lord Krishna to Arjuna, to which dad added Hindi words with the meaning, "we should try and accept this."

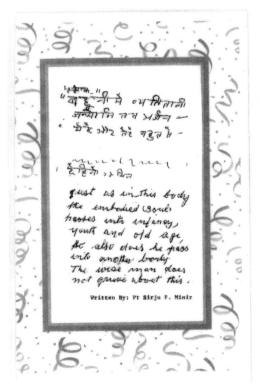

Just as in this body – in our dad's handwriting

Dad also left copies of some of his favourite bhajans such as *bipti me harni* (remover of suffering/calamity), *kab miliye* (when we will meet) and *nirbal ka praan* ...(may the connection between me and the Lord never be broken) neatly written in a new book. Just before his passing, the last book he ordered was - *where are my departed loved ones,* by Swami Paramahamsa Yogananda. Dad was still trying to help his family as he was preparing for his departure.

The peace and fulfilment that our father manifested in life extended to a relative ease with which he passed on. In death too, our father was being rewarded for a life well lived. Whether fortuitously, or by design, family member, Dr. Anand Doobay was in attendance at the hospital's emergency ward on the day of our dad's passing. Through Dr. Anand's influence, our (large) family was allowed unlimited access to our dad's room in the intensive care unit, where we continued singing dhoons (g) by our loved one's side until the end.

Accompanying the family through this period, Dr. Budhendranath Doobay - father of Dr. Anand - and his brother Pt Rabindranauth Doobay, Pt Bhojnarine Sharma of the Vishnu Mandir and Pt Rabindranauth Tiwari offered final prayers. They were shortly joined by family members, Pt Laikram Tiwari and Pt Ramnarine Tiwari. Dr. Budhendranauth, along with Pt Bhojnarine, had also visited our father on the day of the surgery in their role as priests. Their presence provided immense solace to our dad. Both priests had lifelong relationships with our dad and Dr. Doobay's relationship started with his father Pt Ramsahai who mentored dad in the early days of his priesthood.

In life, our father cared about each person. The touching farewell from the people he loved so dearly was a send off in kind; a fitting and beautiful expression of affection in the concluding chapter of his life. Soon after he took the last breath, the family was treated to a broad, ecstatic smile on our dad's face. It seemed a confirmation to the family that their loved one was at great peace, and brought some comfort.

Dr. Budhendranauth, leader and visionary, quick to assess the potential impact and response from the community on our father's passing, volunteered the premises of the Vishnu Mandir as a place for the family to hold the wake. The wake at the Vishnu Mandir—which ran for two nights together with the two nights of viewing at the Elgin Mills Crematorium—saw thousands of people showing up to pay their final respects. At the Vishnu Mandir, members from the temple banded to provide incredible support, ensuring that all who came were comfortably accommodated. This included preparing and serving snacks at the end of each evening. The team provided the Misir family with all the space they needed to grieve in their sudden loss.

At the crematorium, the turnout was so large that many who showed up to offer their last respects left after not being able to get into the compound. Many travelled from Trinidad, Guyana, The United States and various parts of Canada in order to pay their last respects.

At the wake at both venues, many speakers described our dad's humility, kindness and gentleness of spirit. They talked about his dedication to working for the welfare of all, and his belief in surrounding oneself with people of good character.

In our native village of Clonbrook, friends, family and god children gathered at the family home where they sang prayers and talked about our dad's contributions to society. The wake was held each night until the day of the funeral. A memorial was also held in New York, and prayers were offered at many temples in Guyana, Canada and the US.

In the family home in Markham, Canada, the family got together each night until the twelfth day shraadha to offer prayers. Musicians, singers and other members of the community dropped by during the sessions to join in prayers and bhajans and offer support to the family. They included priests from many of the temples in and around the greater Toronto area.

Many from the community brought food for the family, or sent flowers and fresh fruits. Members from the community residing in the United States mailed fresh leaves for the pujas. Phone calls and emails poured in by those touched by our father. Some of the many sentiments expressed in the emails of condolences are reproduced here:

> *I first met the late Pt Sirju Persaud when he got married to my cousin over 60 yrs ago. Even at my young age he struck me as someone who was special. In addition to his leadership and active involvement in the community, he was a kind man who never showed signs of Egoism which is always a Saintly Character.*
>
> – Dr Budhendranauth Doobay, Leader

> *My Guruji – a simple soul, a humble soul, a pure soul. An individual who was always at peace within himself. He never spoke negatively about anyone.*
>
> – Narendra Singh, Godson

> *He always preached to us that with time we will grow to accept this major loss quoting from the Gita, chapter 2, verse 23 – weapons do not cut the soul.*
>
> – Bhowan Maraj, Godson

> *A great soul and a beautiful person.*
>
> – Yasmine Singh, family friend

> *He was a good man, a great man, a fantastic neighbour, a rare individual.*
>
> –RS Singh, Benefactor of the Clonbrook Hindu Temple

> *When a person of character dies, the community suffers; until a replacement is found. Christians, Muslims, all*

showed him reverence. He earned it, it was the best of riches.
  – Meer Khan, former Clonbrook resident

This is a great loss to everyone that knows him and the entire community.
  – Parm Persaud, family friend

He always had a saintly look on his face. When I saw him, I went to him to touch his feet and get his blessings.
  – Rani Sethi, member from Vishnu Mandir

You all suffered the loss of a great father; we lost a great friend/uncle and a very important country man. He was a shining star.
  – Safdar Khan, former Clonbrook resident

Your Dad was a beacon of light to our community.
  – Deo Ramkissoon, family friend

He always emitted that peacefulness and his smile and the way he spoke was very calming.
  – Omo and Latch Persaud, members from Vishnu Mandir

His personality and approach to any situation, religious or otherwise, was always that of excellence and with a smile. His devotion towards the principles and teachings of Sanatan Dharma and to be able to hand down these teachings to younger family members was very important to him. For this, I must say thank you.
  – Deonarine Tiwari, Nephew

A smile that radiated kindness, warmth and friendship that we would miss forever. He was a good listener and always gave good advice to any problem with quotations from the Bhagavad Gita. He always said that every day is a blessing and the fortunate should give freely to the hungry and he will in turn receive.

– Deodharry and Rohini Datt,
brother-in-law and sister-in-law

Your dad was an important person in my life, he was always kind and helpful. He always had a smile on his face and words of encouragement. We talked about many things, religious and non-religious. I learnt from his experiences and understood that a University degree (which I already had) was not everything. All of you can be proud of what your dad accomplished. He was always trying to make his kids better.

– Dr. Neo Sawh, former Clonbrook resident

Since the passing of his jiva atma (g), our dad's life of simplicity and humility has been immortalized at the doorsteps of two of the most popular temples in the greater Toronto area – the Vishnu Mandir and the Devi Mandir. The commemorative plaques installed in his honour at the two institutions underscore our dad's lifelong commitment to the ideals of Sanatan Dharma, and to the promotion of its values. The first commemorative plaque was unveiled by President Amar Binda of the Devi Mandir in Pickering at a special ceremony held at the temple on July 1, 2012. The plaque is located at the wall entrance of the temple.

Devi Mandir Plaque

One would ask the question - what makes our dad stand out to be admired by laymen and academics alike? The most resounding answer would perhaps be - not because he was a great man, but because he was able to see the spark of greatness in each. In life, this was one of his messages.

After the memorial at the Devi Mandir, a one year Varshik Shraddha was performed at the Misir family home in Markham on December 5, 2012. This prayer service is usually done on or around the first death anniversary of a deceased person for the peace of the soul. The prayer service was conducted by the family Priest, Pt Bhojnarine Sharma, with family members, friends and god children of our late dad participating.

Following this event, a four session Bhagavat yajna commenced the next day at the Vishnu Mandir in Richmond Hill. The yajna was presided over by Dr. Budhendranauth Doobay, brother-in-law to our dad. Dr. Doobay treated the congregation to gems from the Bhagavad Gita, one of our dad's favourite texts. In his sermon, Dr. Doobay made supplications for salvation of the soul of the departed. My siblings and the grandchildren joined in rendering a medley of our dad's most cherished songs and prayers. Dhiren Misir, one of the younger grandchildren, performed a rendition of the popular devotional item *Raghupati Raghav Raja Ram* on his guitar. It was one of my father's, as well as Mahatma Gandhi's, favourite bhajans.

At the conclusion of the Yajna, the second commemorative plaque in our dad's honour was unveiled by Chairman Dr. Doobay of the Vishnu Mandir and is now exhibited in the main hallway of the Mandir.

Vishnu Mandir Plaque

This sloka from Ch 2 v 47 of the Bhagavad Gita exemplifies his life: *No matter what conditions you encounter in life, your right is only to the works – not to the fruits thereof*

In January 2013, some members of our family travelled from Canada and the US to our native village of Clonbrook in Guyana to celebrate our dad's life through prayers. The prayer service was presided over by Pt Jaiwant of New York who read from our dad's favourite text, the Bhagavad Gita. A third plaque was unveiled at this location by the Misir family. It described our dad's noble qualities and also included one of his favourite prayers, the Gita Dhyanam. The ceremony concluded with Shiv leading a medley of dad's favourite bhajans.

Clonbrook Plaque

Our father's life of giving and helping the unfortunate continues to be the agenda and mission of his children. Following his passing, Toronto lawyer and community activist, Mr. Dhaman Kissoon, spearheaded and pledged his support towards the setting up of a scholarship fund. Dhaman hails from the neighbouring Bee Hive village, and in his youth accompanied our dad at havan ceremonies in Guyana. He envisioned the scholarship as a means to continue our father's legacy by way of encouraging youths to attain higher education. A result of the initiative was the establishment in 2013 of the Pt Sirju Persaud Misir Scholarship foundation, a program administered by his children and funded by his children, grand children, god children and friends of the family.

The Hindu College, Cove & John, was the first institution selected to be granted the scholarship. Many of Pt Sirju's children attended this institution, which he held dearly. Three children from the school were sponsored for the 2012 – 2014 school years. The family plans to continue to make the scholarships available to a broader segment of the population by seeking and encouraging deserving children who want to pursue higher education, but who don't have the means to do so.

The following Gitanjali quote by Rabindranath Tagore, in our dad's handwriting was found in a religious text he passed on to my brother Pt Jaiwant. It reflected the peace as he prepared to leave.

> "I have got my leave. Bid me farewell, my brothers!
>
> "I bow to you all and take my departure.
>
> "Here I give back the keys of my door and I give up all claims to my house; I only ask for last kind words from you."
>
> "We were neighbours for long, but I received more than I could give.
>
> "Now the day has dawned and the lamp that lit my dark corner is out.
>
> "A summons has come and I am ready for my journey.
>
> *Gitanjali*

Our dad's soul may have moved on but his legacy continues to live on and inspire his family and the many people whose lives he has touched. He gave generously of everything in his possession, asking for nothing in return. Our hope is that our dear beloved dad will forever live in our hearts to inspire us to continue to be better individuals and see that spark of divinity in all creation.

To our father:

> *You are gone from this physical world but never from our hearts. Our wish for you is that you will be cradled in the arms of the Lord and you will enjoy peace, bliss and eternal love. Just as your memory will live forever, so does our love for you.*

Appendix 1

Chelas' Tributes

Pt Sirju's relationships with his chelas were that of a kind father protecting, guiding, and encouraging his children. As with the other aspects of his life, he humbly accepted the guru role as a great honour, whereby he was offered a unique opportunity to impart his wisdom and knowledge to the youths. It was another manifestation of his empathy with everyone he met. Tributes from 4 of his godchildren are included here.

Godson Ramraj Singh
The words of his GodSon Ramraj Singh echo the loving relationship he maintained with his chelas:

> *Memories of my Guruji: My Hero, The late Pandit Sirju Persaud Misir.*
> It was 1954 when my Mom and Dad told me that it was time for me to have my Janeo done, and for me to get a godfather (guru). That was a very important time for me as an eleven year old, and I took my parents' suggestion very seriously. With all humility, I asked if I could choose my guru. My dad enquired whom I wanted to be my guru. I told him that there was a pandit from Clonbrook who was an insurance agent and whom I liked a lot. He was young (about 30), very good-looking and handsome, he was always well dressed, and I liked how he did his pujas. Also I never heard anyone say any bad things about him.

My dad asked if I was talking about Pandit Lionel (Sirju), and I answered in the affirmative. My parents supported my choice and I was a very happy young man. One afternoon a few days later, my Dad took me to Clonbrook where we met Pandit Sirju in his shop. Of course, we were greeted warmly with that smile and cordial demeanor. My Dad told Pandit Sirju that it was my desire for him to do my Janeo and to be my Guru. Panditji consented and expressed his pleasure that I chose him to be my Guru. I am not sure if I was the first "chela" of Pandit Sirju, if not, I was among his first five. Of course, later that year the Janeo was done, and I was blessed with the best Guru anyone could have had. This also heralded a fairy-tale relationship between a Guru and his "chela".

The choice of Pandit Sirju Persaud Misir (Pandit Lionel) as my Guru was a very easy one for me. He stood out as an individual whom you could not help but like. As I said before, he was young, good-looking, soft spoken with a win-some smile which greeted everyone he met. In my mind, I needed a Guru who would be there for me for a very long time. In those days people chose pundits who were in their senior years as gurus. After a while, those pundits passed on and the "chelas" were left with only the memories and teachings of their gurus. After 58 years I realized how correct and fortunate I was in choosing Pandit Sirju as my Guru.

My three brothers one deceased, and some of my cousins are also chelas of PanditJi.

As my Guru, I looked up to PanditJi. We kept in touch with each other while in Guyana, and of course, he was there to officiate at our Jhandis and other pujas. Whenever we met he would always offer me and the family words of encouragement. A few times he even advised me to change my habits that were inimical to my well-being.

When my wife and I migrated to Minnesota, USA in 1974, communication with Guruji was limited. However, when Guruji and Mataji moved to Canada we resumed close relationship and kept in touch on a regular basis. In 1990 our son David was 12 years old, and it was his turn for Janeo sanskar and to have his Guru. With our input, David chose Guru Bhai, Pandit Jaiwant Persaud Misra to be his Guru. To celebrate David's sanskar (Janeo) and to give thanks to Bhagwan for all the blessings we enjoyed over the years, we invited our Guruji to officiate at a Three Day Ramayan Yagna at our home in Apple Valley, Minnesota. This yagna was significant because it was the very first yagna done in Minnesota. Pandit Sirju officiated Friday and Saturday evenings, and Pandit Jaiwant officiated on Sunday.

To put it mildly, my Guruji and I had a very close relationship. Our calls to each other were frequent. Sometimes when I felt a bit "down" I would call just to hear his sweet voice. His voice lifted me up and provided me with the serenity that one gets after pujas and prayers at a mandir. If for some reason I did not call my Guruji, I will get a call from him enquiring how I was doing. Of course, it was always special when I called him on his birthday, Father's Day, New Year's Day, Diwali and Holi. I am told that his eyes would light up whenever he heard that I was on the line waiting to talk with him. Whenever my wife, Rukhmin and I visited their home in Toronto, Guruji and Mataji would greet us warmly, offer us a meal or snacks and say a prayer with us before we departed.

Guruji did not only focus his attention on me, he always enquired about my wife, Rukhmin and our children, Andrea and David and their families. He had a close relationship with my 89 year old Mom whom he called a couple of weeks before his passing.

I was very fortunate to see my Guruji for the last time when Guru Bhai, Anant Misir and Bahin Radica and family sponsored a Three Day Yagna in New York in October, 2011. As I left the mandir when the yagna concluded the Sunday afternoon, we hugged each other and he wished me well. Little did I know it was the last hug I would receive from my beloved Guruji.

My GuruJi was awesome. He was a great mentor whose life was an example for all to follow. He worked hard, was a great husband, father, grandfather, father-in-law, brother, guru, teacher, friend and neighbor. He cared about everyone regardless of race, age, religion, sex or political persuasion. A huge part of his life was spent helping people and building communities in Guyana and Canada. This world is a better place and I am a better person because of my GuruJi, and I will forever be grateful to him.

I enjoyed my GuruJi for 58 years and I will always keep him in my thoughts and prayers. He is gone but not forgotten. I know that he is listening to my daily prayers and will continue to lift me up and keep me under his wings.

My Guru and God stand before me.
Whose feet must I touch first?
At your feet do I bow GuruJi,
Since I know God only by your teaching."

Godson Pt Eshwar Persaud Doobay wrote:

Two decades ago in Toronto I reconnected with my God Father Pt. Sirju Persaud Misir and immediately felt fortunate and blessed, as so much to say, I constantly give thanks to my parents that they saw it fit to select and appoint such a fine, distinguished, charismatic individual to be our God Father. As far back in Guyana and Toronto as I can remember he was always the family priest and my parents and entire family adored him. He at all times carried the order of a priest in the most highest and dedicated spiritual manner performing his responsibilities dharmically. My relationship with him was more like a father and son, we travelled and attended many spiritual functions together and we had numerous conversations on a variety of topics which acted as a spiritual catalyst for me. My God Father was indeed a humble, simple, but a man of significant intellectual depth with great mannerism, and a jovial, humorous personality. He has left a significant and indelible impression on me and it is difficult to fill the hole in my heart by the passing of my God Father. I will always treasure the time I spent with him.

Godson Vishnu S. Jagroo of Bee Hive wrote these words:

A cherished love the Vishnu families have accumulated since our association with the pious soul the late guru Sirju Persaud. Fortunately our guru for 51 years, who has captivated the hearts of the Vishnu family and thousands of persons who he came into contact with from all ethnic groups, during his life time. Physically Guru Sirju died, but spiritually he continues to live. He will be forever remembered, as he left a legacy of love for us to ponder.

The name of our Guru shall be written in the book of memory in letters of gold, that cannot be erased and would pass on through generations, so that whoever reads the pages, would be happy to know the ancestors they came from, that a personality such as Guru Sirju walked on this land of Clonbrook and elsewhere in flesh and left behind his footprints for others to follow.

'Lead us from darkness to light'. Nevertheless if your guru is no more, the mantra lives on until the end of time. So this pedestal is reserved for our wonderful Guru. Whose blessings we are fortunate to have. Finally if we are fortunate to be reborn as human, our first wish is to be born back as the chela (god child) of this most inspired Guru.

Godson, Bhose Harripaul wrote of his relationship:

My Guruji, was a pillar of strength, wealth of knowledge, embodiment of peace and a champion of Sanatan Dharma. I am the third generation in the family who was associated with the late Pandit Sirju Persaud Misir. I remember him as a humble, simple, knowledgeable and spiritual person who had an enormous influence and impact on my life. As a young boy, I recall attending the Clonbrook Hindu temple where I was taught Hindi, obedience and other religious duties from him, something I cherish and continue to advance throughout my life. I attended his religious services, pujas, kathas, and yajnas and other spiritual functions that he officiated and I grew fascinated with his depth of knowledge about Hinduism and other religions. His devotion and commitment to Hinduism allowed him to travel throughout the vast coastline of Guyana and later in life Trinidad and Canada, inspiring the lives of devotees with his knowledge. His teachings and encouragement to young children were remarkable, as he always made himself available for discussions about the Hindu religion and whatever adversity affected you, in spite of the demands of his family and personal life.

During one of his many religious services at our home, I was fortunate to become one of his god children. His advice and encouragement greatly shaped my life for the future. After I immigrated to Canada and got married I remembered his words of wisdom before my departure: be honest, truthful and remember your religion, your Dharma. You will accomplish your goal no matter what obstacles or insecurities you experience.

When he and his family immigrated to Canada I was fortunate to have him at my home officiating at a religious ceremony and at that time my wife also became his god child. During his lifetime I continued to seek his advice, knowledge about Hinduism and his blessings.

His passing was a personal loss for me and my family; we will miss him and forever remember him for his advice, kindness, generosity and wisdom and for being our godfather. He left in our thoughts a lasting impression and legacy to all who knew, revered and immortalised him.

May Bhagwan Shri Ram accept his soul in his golden chariot.

Appendix 2

Contributors

Dalia Persaud
Dr B.N. Kumar
Walter Dipchand
Pt Bhojnarine Sharma
Dhaman Kissoon
Lakharam Jaipargas
Nandram Kissoon
Pt Sukhdeo Maharaj
Pt Dr Latchman P. Kissoon
Ramrattie Mohamaid
Ramraj Singh
Shanti Edun
Jayt Jugmohan
Deodharry & Rohini Datt
Pt Ramnarine Tiwari
Liloutie (Leila) Ramsaywack
Prabhudyal Beepatnath (Chili)
Dr Budhendranauth Doobay
Pt Omanand Persaud
Swami Bhajananda
Chandranarain Doobay (Cecil Ram)
Basmatie (Prandai Singh)
Chantamonie Minkoo
Dolly Panday
Sudama Singh
Sylvie Falk
Sattebhama Doodnauth
Balram Brijmongal
Bhowan Maraj
Rani Sethi
Omo & Latch Persaud
Dewan Singh
Raghu & Yvonne Chintaram
Dhiren Misir
Tiya Misir
Hemant Misir
Akshay Misir
Shivaal Misir
Shiv Misir
Somant Maraj
Hardeep Maraj
Dr Tishan Maraj
Jitin Maraj
Dr Youtradeo Maraj
Basso Maraj
Parbatee Persaud
Pt Jaiwant Misir
Dhanesh Misir
Anant Misir
Natasha Misir
Darshanand Rampersaud
Yudhisthir Rampersaud
Chandra Rampersaud
Deodat Tiwari
Roger Rajkumar
Thakur Persaud
Meer Khan
P. P. Shivraj
Ravi Sharma
Pt Rabindranauth Tiwari
Yasmine Singh
Safdar Khan
Pammy Khan
Joan Bajnauth
Pt Somdath Padarath

Lochan Nandram	Jhawanti Ramnarain	R. S. Singh
Narendra Datt	Basmattie Doobay	Pt Laikram Tiwari
Kaywala Persaud	Deonarine Tiwari	Umesh Singh
Khemraj Persaud	Raj Persaud	Narendra Singh
Sachin Persaud	Amar Binda	Parm Persaud
Divya Persaud	Gangadei Hemraj	Deo Ramkissoon
Ravi Misir	Vishnu S Jagroo	Jasodra Raghunandan
Harold Kowlessar	Jagnandan family	Pt Inderpaul Tiwari
Bhose Harripaul	Raghnauth Singh	Chaitram Manaram
Betty Singh	Dr Neo Sawh	
Dhori Raghunauth	Ravendra Kowlessar	
Narine Gangadin	Pt Eshwar Doobay	

APPENDIX 3

Glossary

Achaar	- Spicy pickled vegetables or fruits used as a condiment with snacks or food
Aarti	- Part of Hindu worship where worship while singing prayers to the deities are done with lighted wicks or camphor
Aja	- Father's dad
Backdam	- Farmland in deep rural areas in Guyana
Bara	- A mixture of ground peas or chickpeas with flour and spices rolled out into thin circles and fried until golden brown
Badam lachha	- A flaky, stringy dessert made from flower, sugar and ghee
Baraat	- Bridegroom's procession to the Hindu wedding venue
Baraatis	- Invitees who accompany the wedding procession
Beta	- Son
Bhajan	- Any song that expresses love for the Divine
Bora	- A long green bean
Cake shop	- Term used to describe a store that sold cakes, soft drinks, and assorted snacks
Camoudie	- South American python
Chacha	- Father's brother

Chandan	- Sandalwood powder made into a paste and applied to the forehead
Chela	- God child who is required to pay reverence to his/her godfather
Chowpaees	- Stanzas from the holy texts usually narrated with a melody
Chowtal	- A special form of singing associated with the colourful Holi festival
Courida	- Trees that grow by the seashore
Daubing	- Applying a mixture of mud and water to the ground
Devotees	- Worshippers
Dharampatni	- Wife
Dharma	- The path of righteousness, living according to the Divine law of the Lord as per the Hindu Scriptures
Dharmacharya	- One who follows Dharma, the path of righteousness
Dhoti	- Traditional men's garment comprising of a rectangular piece of cloth wrapped around the waist and legs before being tied into a knot at waist
Dhoons	- Religious songs
Fire baba	- One who makes the offerings into the fire during the Hindu Ceremony
Gaff	- Guyana slang for chat
Gana	- Marriage compatibility
Ganga Ma	- The sacred Ganges river is worshipped as Ganga Ma
Ghazals	- Special poetic songs, of devotion, love and beauty
Greenheart	- Wood used to make houses; 50 year life span
Ground provision	- Vegetables that are planted in the ground such as eddoes, cassava and yams

Guru	- Revered Godfather in the Hindu faith, he gives a secret mantra to his chela upon initiation and becomes his spiritual advisor and mentor
Havan	- Offerings into the consecrated fire
Heap	- A heap of dirt burnt at high temperatures to make bricks
Holi	- Spring festival of colours
Imli	- A ritual in the Hindu wedding ceremony in which bride's and groom's maternal uncles participate
Jahaji	- Travelers who arrived by boat from India to the Caribbean
Janeo Samskaar	- Observed between the ages of seven and fourteen, and signifies coming of age of a young man from boyhood. The priest(s) bestow the young man with a sacred thread amidst prayers for blessings. The blessings are to guide in his education, both academic and spiritual, the main pre-occupation in this phase of his life. The janeo ceremony is usually accompanied, but not always, by a 'christening', where a guru is chosen to be a spiritual leader to the young man
Jhandi	- A prayer ceremony worshipping the deity Hanumanji
Jiva atma	- The individual soul
Juwat	- Contraption to attach two bulls to a plow or a rake, used in preparing the soil for rice planting
Kala pani	- Literally meaning 'black water', it refers to a taboo of ancient India that ascribes pollution of caste and assignment of social stigma to someone who crossed its borders via the sea

Kauravas	- Children of Dhritarashtra, older son of the legendary king Kuru. Characters in the Mahabharata, contained in the Bhagavad Gita
Krishna	- See Lord Krishna
Kirtan	- Devotional songs usually sung in accompaniment with instruments such as the harmonium, tabla, drum and dantaal
Kurta	- A long loose fitting shirt with long sleeves worn by men
Lord Krishna	- One of the most commonly worshipped deities in the Hindu faith
Lota	- Brass cup
Lucknie	- A person, usually an older woman who accompanies the bride to the groom's home on the wedding night; a chaperone
Madaar	- Fragrant white or lavender flower, grows in a cluster and usually used to make garlands
Mahabharat	- Major Sanskrit epic of ancient India
Mala	- Garland of flowers
Mamoo	- Mother's brother
Mangrove	- Trees and shrubs that grow in salty water along the coast
Mantras	- Sacred word, syllable or group of words
Masaal	- A usual accompaniment to the coleman lamp used in those days, and consisted of a long stick, to which a kerosene-soaked bag was attached at one end and set ablaze
Maticore	- Special occasion prior to Hindu wedding in the Caribbean where the prospective groom and bride are prepared for the upcoming nuptials, including being rubbed down with turmeric
Mathya/Mandir	- A Hindu Temple / Place of worship
Mauby	- Drink made from steeping bark of mauby tree and sweetened, served with ice. The tree

	is native to northern Caribbean and South Florida
Middle walk	- The long trench and surrounding areas running along the middle of Clonbrook village connecting residential area with the savannahs
Mitthai	- Indian sweets made from flour, margarine and coconut, that are rolled, cut and deep fried before being coated with syrup
Mohan bhog	- Dessert made from flour, ghee, milk and raisins which is offered to The Lord
Mousie	- Mother's sister
Murtis	- Images that express a divine spirit
Nana	- Mother's father
Nani	- Mother's mother
Neiba	- Guyanese creole word for neighbour
Nine day	- Celebration that occurs on the ninth day after the birth of a newborn
Nowah	- The person who helps to prepare the puja area and assemble all the items needed for the Hindu rituals
Nowraat	- Special period of nine nights designated for worshipping the Divine Mother
Pandavas 1	- The male participants in a Yajna. They usually partake in the fire Rituals
Pandavas 2	- Children of Pandu, younger son of the legendary king Kuru. Characters in the Mahabharata, contained in the Bhagavad Gita
Pandit	- Hindu priest
Parche	- Greeting the groom upon his arrival at the wedding venue with a lighted wick
Patra	- Used by Hindu Priest to forecast the future based on birth sign, to select names for newborn, dates for marriages and successful ventures

Pera	- A round shaped fudge, made from milk and sugar
Phuwa	- Father's sister
Pitagee	- Dear respected father
Prasad	- Made with flour, sugar and milk, and used as offerings in pujas and all prayers
Puja	- Hindu Prayer service
Puri	- Dough made from flower that are rolled into thin circles and deep fried in vegetable oil or ghee (clarified butter)
Purple heart	- Wood used to make inside construction for homes; similar but a softer wood type than greenheart
Ragas	- Varied styles of Indian classical music
Ramayana	- One of the great epics of Hinduism
Ramayana goal	- Group that chants from the holy Ramayana text
Rishis	- Sages or saints
Sadhu	- A good man who aims to advance spiritually
Salara	- Roll made with red coloured coconut
Samaji	- An Arya Samaj devotee
Sanatan dharma	- Another name for Hinduism
Satsang	- Praying, singing bhajans or meditating in a group
Savannahs	- The land extending from the residential to the conservancy was collectively and colloquially referred to as savannahs; the first parts, consisting of cultivation area were cleared and technically were now farmland
Singhasan	- A special decorative podium, it is elevated and is built with a comfortable seat for the Pandit to sit on when officiating at a Yajna
Sohar	- Special folk song, usually sung at nine day celebrations
Sloka	- Verse in Hindu religious text

Surujnarayan	- Worship of the Sun
Swami	- A Hindu religious teacher or saint
Tabla	- A set of two hand drums that are played by one person
Tassa	- A type of drum commonly played at Hindu weddings
Trench	- River, but usually smaller in width and depth than a river
Trust	- Colloquial term used to indicate that the bill incurred will be paid later, and the requestor should be 'trusted' to do pay
Vedic	- According to the Vedas, a large body of Sanskrit texts that are the oldest scriptures of Hindusim, and originating in ancient India
Wallaba	- Wood used to make fences, posts; had 5-10 year span
Yajman	- Host of the puja or ceremony